STEVEN SLATEST
WHAT IN THE WORLD IS GOING ON HERE?

CONTENTS

INTRODUCTION

What's going on around here? Ever find yourself asking that question? In my world, it's a question that's asked every day. I myself ask it every time I read a paper (yes, I still read a paper!), or watch a feed from my phone or office computer. And aren't phones dandy? I now have access to frustration, uncertainty, and just plain old anger at any given moment. I have alerts that will keep me up to the minute with the latest outrage or lunatic on the loose. Aren't we lucky! Sure it's cool to get updates on my beloved Yankees or Giants, but most of my updates just carry bad news. Frightening news at times. Well sure, I can always turn off these notifications, but who wants to feel out of the loop or uninformed.

Being an educator of high-school age students, I feel a responsibility to stay informed and able to discuss with my students the issues pertinent to all of our lives. Sometimes this is done with ease, other times not so easy. How do you get teenagers engaged in the world outside social media and their immediate surroundings? Some say, why should they become engaged? Some feel that perhaps they are too young to be concerned by what's going on around them, I disagree. Our kids are more sophisticated than ever, and can have a better understanding of the issues that face us in today's volatile world, if I can only get them to put down that dam phone!

Many adults get their info on what's going on around the world straight from Facebook or other social-media news outlets as well. They all have very different answers to the question, what's going on around here? Just ask someone if they use CNN or Fox News as their news source and you know all you need to know about them, right?? We are living in what I believe is the most divisive society in the past 50 years. I was too young to fully realize the divisiveness of the civil-rights era of the 1960's, so I have never witnessed this extent of polarization. Many issues divide us today; rich vs poor, the disappearing middle class, immigration, terrorism, law-enforcement, poverty and education, and just plain politics. Let's not leave out the issues of racial and gender inequality. I can now hear the politically correct police saying, "..hey, what about my issue?" The LGBT movement... Animal rights... and the millennial's screaming about not winning or receiving a trophy today. I can't address all of our society's issues, everyone one of them is worthy,(well with the exception of the millennials), so I will choose what I see as the most impactful. Impactful to me, and I am sure for many others as well.

I usually like to get both sides of an issue then commit to a position. A position that can always change as circumstances changes. Most of my positions come from my upbringing. I was born and raised in the Bronx, son of an NYPD officer. I went to Catholic schools, and the neighborhood I grew up in was a mixture of white, black, Jewish and Hispanic. I had many friends, most of their names ended in vowels, but I was raised in a diverse area and learned from that as I got older. The Bronx in the 1960s, '70s and '80s was a great place to grow up. I have many wonderful memories from that time. I was raised in what was then a middle-class upbringing. We didn't have all that we wanted, but we had all that we needed to succeed as adults. Never hungry, filled with hope, but definitely not without its pratfalls. Drugs, violence, economic hardships, all plagued our neighborhood from time to time. Friends were killed, some got hooked on drugs. Others fell into a life of crime. Some of these issues touched my family as well. But still, many of us went on to get a job and raise families of our own. But in a very different world. All of this within a short period of time. One lifetime. My own. And here's the deal; it is changing at a rate which has not been seen so far in my lifetime. The 21st century is into its second decade, and there is so much to discuss already.

The issues that I discuss are not in any particular order of importance. Quite frankly, I've never written a book before, and the issues came to me randomly. And get this, sometimes the issues overlap each other. Now I'm sure I have left out info and will piss off people in the process. But all in all, sit back, open your mind to both sides and enjoy the ride in what has been a flying start to the 21st century.

CHAPTER ONE

Jihadism

Why not start with a hot topic right out of the box, and start with a definition. Terrorism, (the tactic used most by jihadists), is a modus operandi in which deliberate violence against civilians is used for the purpose of achieving political goals. Whew! Work for you? Works for me. Now comes the wordy part. There are many types of terror groups; there are anarchists, anti-globalist, communist/socialist, racist, religious, and let's throw in right-wing groups as well. A high level of concern is seen when terrorists are motivated by what they see as a religious mission. Killing people, blowing themselves up, all in the name of their god, whoever they say it is. Recently, it has been Allah. Let's not pussyfoot around here. Modern day terrorism is perceived to be predominantly perpetrated by those who feel they are doing this in the name of Allah. Islamic terrorism. They regard themselves as being a messenger of god. Tough work, huh? The only objective here seems to be to engage in an all-out war against the

infidels. And since I am one of those so-called infidels, I take this person-
ally and seriously, as should all infidels who live in the U.S of A. Some of
the groups associated with modern day terrorism are: Al-Qaeda, Taliban,
ISIS (or whatever initials our leaders are using to identify this group). Let's
throw in Hezbollah and Hamas as well.

But who belongs to these groups? Who exactly is trying to create fear
and anxiety within in a society? Are they a bunch of crazy people randomly
attacking the west? Well, when you take a deeper look into what goes on in
creating these attackers, you see a more devious and a more undetectable
portrait emerge. Those who have studied these groups debunk the notion
that these groups are made up of crazy people. But when you look at one
of the techniques used by terror groups today, the suicide bomber, if not
crazy, what the hell are they?

A portrait emerges showing someone who has made a "rational"
decision: Someone who thinks that terrorism outweighs any other alternative; someone who feels that it is the most effective way to achieve their
political goals, and let's not leave out, it's also their best way to leave a mark,
go out with a bang, so to speak. How do you get a person to make a "rational" decision to wrap a bomb around themselves and kill innocent people
and themselves in the process?

Most suicide bombers are "self-starters," not the brainwashed sheep
that most people think they are. It seems that when looking at this group
more closely, they are neither "suicidal nor homicidal" maniacs. Suicide
bombers don't seem to be the poor and ignorant dupes as we suspected
they were. Nor are they overly oppressed with no future. And in fact, most
suicide bombers are not even religious fanatics. Common characteristics of the "suicide bomber"are: alienation, possessing a sense of injustice,
searching for adventure, and having a strong need for recognition. Wow,
that helps. Shouldn't be hard to identify that group, huh? So basically, what
the experts are saying is that anyone, under the right circumstances, can

become a card-carrying suicide bomber. Don't know about you, but this shit just got serious.

Let's take a look at radicalization here in our great country. People who have been recently radicalized seem to know very little about Islam. You can also call it a "youth" movement. Not too many 60-year-old jihadists in our midst. These isolated, self-righteous, adventure seeking, disenfranchised youth are told an Islamic religious tale of "Jihad". Many are not from American-Muslim communities. This is not a Muslim uprising here in the U.S. Many "jihadists" are not poverty stricken or oppressed at all. But most do carry with them this "rebel without a cause" complex. For the convert, the only way religion plays into this form of radicalization is that it offers a person a way to restructure their life. It changes their name from Billy or Susie to Mohid or Aiza. It changes the way you dress, going from khakis and flip-flops to burqas or hijabs. It puts the new recruit more in line with the "truth". They can now say they have a higher purpose! In fact, their motives are not altruistic, but instead, very personal in nature. They can be considered spoiled and overindulgent youth rebelling against society.

When looking at suicide bombers as a whole, they are comprised of either, recent converts (American born citizens), and/or 2nd or 3rd generation Muslims living in our country. These young men and women are not looking to other family members when radicalizing. It is certainly not a family affair. Actually, it's quite the opposite. Many begin a process of dropping out of conventional society. Leaving their social cliques, abandoning their school/work groups or teams. They step away from friends and girlfriends/boyfriends. A charismatic leader will emerge to isolate the recruit. The recruiters look to downsize their social contacts. Limit them to a small group. Typically, you hear after the fact that they withdrew from family and friends. They started to spend unusual amounts of time alone in their rooms on the computer, started to dress differently and took on a new persona.

The process begins. The fresh recruit is fed a barrage of imagery that looks to dehumanize the "enemy". When you wonder how someone can walk into a crowd and blow up innocent people along with themselves, well, by this point they don't see human life as most others do. They see their victims as the "oppressors", not their next-door neighbors or former friends. The job of the recruiter is to get these potential jihadists ready to die for the "cause". This new cause is quite new to them, it energizes them and propels them to become a believer.

As with most young people I have interacted with in my twenty plus years as a high-school social studies teacher, there is an absence of political sophistication. The worldly views that can come with adulthood have not been attained as of yet. The recruiter preys on this inexperience and fills it with a false narrative, one that is readily digested by this easy-to-assemble group of potential jihadist weaponry! The young are heavily influenced by propaganda. Well, to be honest, who isn't? When vulnerable people are fed info that makes sense to them, true or not, it will produce responses that fall in line with the propagandists. People who are ready to hear a message, will swallow whole whatever is being fed to them. They are a willing and ready-made audience.

Most experts now believe the speed to being radicalized is much swifter than first thought. It doesn't take years or months to get the job done. We are talking weeks to produce a bomb carrying jihadist. And we thought they could never account for much. Young people today lack motivation and discipline, huh? We have to revisit this point of view perhaps. Anyone can be motivated if ready. Isolate them, put them in front of a computer, and saturate their minds with visions of greatness, immortality, and there you have it; a motivated teenager or millennial! Imagine that.

When dealing with 2nd or 3rd generational jihadists, we look at what are called "push" factors. Basically, what pushed these Muslim-Americans to become radicalized? As it turns out, they don't always see the world as their parents or grandparents do. Hmm, again, imagine that! This group of potential jihadists might have experienced resentments stemming from incidents of racism. They might have been made fun of or worse for being different. Now the cynic in me might say, "Hey hasn't every newly arrived immigrant group experienced this type of bullying and overt racism"? The Irish, the Italians, the newly arrived Hispanic groups? But it seems with this group there is another layer of underlying resentment that is ready to emerge and emerge in a very violent way. Biting the hand that feeds them. Their families came here to escape oppressive poverty only to have their sons and daughters act out violently towards the country that gave them their chance for a new life.

Usually, the Muslim-American jihadist has experienced some type of personal failure, perhaps at school or at the workplace. Or they didn't live up to their or their parent's expectations. As with every passing generation, there is a battle between the old and the new. I used to be the new, now I find myself on the side of the old. Funny how that works. One day you are shaking your head over something your parents said or did; the next day you see your kids shaking their heads at you. And usually over the same thing! This is an age-old dynamic. A rite of passage. I'm sure everyone reading this has experienced this to some extent. How many of us have strapped a bomb to our bodies and killed innocent people along with ourselves? Never mind, don't answer that. But I would put the answer at a ridiculously low number.

Unfortunately, the tensions felt in the Muslim-American communities between the old and the new are producing suicide bombers and that's scary. It's not really hard to decipher. The old are stuck in the ways of their homeland. They are steeped in their religious and political ways of the past. Their social customs are also from that past. Their bodies are here, but their hearts and souls reside in their past. This is frustrating to the young, the new. They seek alternatives. They want a more modern, more politicized, less religious approach to life. What young Muslim-Americans experience is that the old shun our politics and they want the new to follow them. But kids being kids....

The young develop a "new" style of worship. More modern, and dare say, more western. They want to apply a more aggressive political agenda. Become more relevant and part of the discussion. They also want to step away from old religious practices like say, arranged marriages. They want to select their own partners. And aghast, be their homosexual selves if that's the case. All of which is obviously blasphemous to the older crowd. Also, get this, the younger crowd wants to have a nightlife. Perhaps drink a bit or indulge in soft drug use. Another shocker, huh? But this is a monumental shift between old and new within the Muslim-American communities. The young are looking to someone to fill this leadership void. They are looking for someone to respect, someone who speaks their language.

And to fill this void is the clever and patient recruiter, hitting all the notes and feeding one very distinct narrative. "Muslims all over the world are under attack. And the blame for this lies at the feet of the West and their allies." This narrative states that it is the duty of every Muslim to fight back. To wreak havoc on the west and to create chaos and fear throughout. This narrative reveals to the disenfranchised young the "truth". But perhaps more importantly, it also provides that person with a solution, a so-called plan of action. For all of this to be accomplished, the recruiter exploits their lack of knowledge in Islam and in world affairs.

The recruiters employ very modern techniques to inspire a "virtual Ummah," or community. Make no mistake about it, this is a very modern movement. It would have to be to catch the attention of our youth. The very group that is most associated with a virtual world. The kids who are always glued to their phones. This generation carry's out most of their social inter-actions through social media. They have no problem communicating with each other online, but falter when face to face. I've seen this and have witnessed this in both my classrooms and in my home. This generation is quite comfortable living in a social media environment and avoiding actual face-to-face social interactions. And hey, if we know it, make pretty dam sure the ISIS recruiter does as well.

Fact is, ISIS uses a very powerful media and propaganda platform. They utilize chat rooms and YouTube recruiting videos, all professionally shot and edited for dramatic effect. This brings recruits and recruiters from all over the world into a small heavily controlled virtual society. A society masterfully orchestrated by terror organizations. Once exposed to this new and exciting social environment, the recruit will begin to fall out of conventional society. Goodbye friends and family of old. Hello to all my new and exciting friends. For some recruits, they never had real friends. Now they do! It's easy to be part of the group, just say and believe as they do. Follow the leader, they will show you the "truth"! The recruits need very little actual knowledge of events as they unfold in places such as Syria or Iraq. They will come to live in their own newly created reality, a reality whereby they get to be the hero, perpetrate violence, and GET HEADLINES!

But now folks, I caution those who would paint all Muslims living in America with broad strokes. By doing this doing , you only add to the terror recruiters' arsenal. It plays into the narrative that all Muslims are persecuted and gives an added motive for revenge. In other words, it is a sure-fire way to stoke the flames of radicalization. So if all Muslims are not terrorists, then who in fact are they? What do you know about the religion of Islam and Muslims as a whole? To start, there are a whole lot of people in this world practicing this religion and identifying themselves as Muslim. In fact, there are over 1.6 billion people worldwide who identify themselves as Muslim. To put that into perspective, that's 23% of the world's population.

Islam is the second largest religion practiced worldwide. It trails only Christianity, which is practiced by 31% of the world population. Islam is also the fastest growing religion worldwide, and it is believed that if it continues to grow at the current rate, it will surpass Christianity by the end of this century! Two logical factors come into focus. First off, Muslims have more children then members of other religious groups. 3.1 children for

Muslim families, 2.3 for all other religions combined. Second, Muslims are the youngest of all religious groups. The average age for a Muslim in 2010 was 23 years old. So when you combine a younger population with a high fertility rate, the reasons for its rapid growth becomes clearer.

Let's look at the Muslim population here in the U.S.. Recent census information shows there are 3.3 million Muslims of all ages living here in our country. That is less than 1% of our total population. Best estimates show that by 2050 that percentages will rise to over 2%. A small percentage, indeed, but it would in fact, surpass the Jewish faith and become the second largest religion practiced in our country. There has also been an increase in Muslim citizenship over the past twenty years. In 1992 we had 5% Muslims living in our country with green cards. By 2012 that percentage has doubled to 10%. On the average, there are approximately 100,000 newly arrived Muslim immigrants per year. This represents about 10% of all legal immigrants arriving in the U.S. each year. Interestingly, most Muslim-Americans fall in line with Christians who live here in the U.S. when you look at religious issues as well as social issues.

A look at recent statistics shows that both groups share roughly the same views on several different religious topics;

- **Religion being important in their lives**:
  - Both groups show that 70% have a belief in a God
  - In both groups, about 65 % pray daily
  - Both groups show approximately 47% attend religious services regularly.
  - Further analysis shows that Muslim-Americans are far less religious than other Muslims who live throughout the world.

- **Social issues:**
  - **Homosexuality**: 45% Muslim-Americans believe it should be socially acceptable; 54% Christians.

- **Same-Sex Marriages:** Muslim-Americans – 42% favor, 52% oppose; Christians – 44% favor, 48% oppose.

- **Abortion**: 55% of Muslim-Americans say it should be legal, 37% illegal; Christians - 47% legal, 48% illegal.

- **Women in the workplace.** Both groups have almost identical percentages 67% favor, 10% unfavorable.

But here's is the twist. When you ask Americans how they view Muslims, you get a completely different picture. Almost 50% of Americans polled thought that Muslim-Americans were anti-American. Half thought Muslims were violent, "fanatical," and need more scrutiny than other groups of people. When you ask Muslim-Americans, they find other Americans to be selfish, greedy, immoral and violent. There certainly is a disconnect between the two groups. While in actuality we see that both groups share many similar views, it is also clear that the feelings between these groups tell quite a different story. Both sides show huge amounts of both ignorance and intolerance, which unfortunately leads to fear and eventually violence.

Back to American radicalization. There have been 352 people in the U.S. charged with some sort of jihadist crime since September 11, 2001. Out of this group, 268 were U.S. citizens. That's over 75% folks. To break it down further, the average age for these terrorists was 29, 37% were married, 93% were male. These are your typical American terrorists. They are Americans terrorists hiding in plain sight.

The American jihadist is both educated and emotionally stable, or as emotionally stable as the rest of us that is. In many instances, there were no outward signs of distress. The type of distress that would eventually translate to unspeakable violence against fellow Americans all in the name of jihad. One of the most dangerous of these American jihadist's was a man by the name of Anwar al-Awlaki.

Awlaki was an American cleric born in April of 1971 to Yemini parents in Las Cruces, New Mexico. At an early age his family moved back to Yemen. His father was a Professor and also the Minister of Agriculture for Yemen. Alwaki moved back to the U.S. as a young adult, to pursue his own college education in 1991. His studies took him to Colorado State to get a B.S. in Civil Engineering, San Diego State to get a Master's in Education, and eventually George Washington University where he attended a PhD Human Resources program.

Background on this character Awlak shows that he has an arrest record for soliciting prostitutes in San Diego. The first time in 1996 then again in 1997. Now I am not saying that this particular behavior makes you a terrorist, but it certainly goes against the preaching of his faith. A faith that he staunchly spewed to his followers and recruits worldwide on the internet. When he was under surveillance by the FBI after the 9/11 attacks, they cited many visits made to motels for rendezvous with prostitutes. Records show that in September of 2001, Awlaki was an Imam at Dar Al-Hijrah, a large mosque in Falls Church, Virginia. But this didn't seem to slow down his appetite for prostitutes. He was also a husband and a father of three at this time. He recorded his sermons and they ended up in the homes of the devout. He was regularly referred to as a spiritual adviser. For a man in this position, his actions were extremely reckless. We have all seen what a sex scandal can do to a religious career?

Awlaki was violating the moral tenets of conservative Islam that he so vehemently preached to his many followers. Not to mention spending money his family did not have. He would spend $300 to $400 for an hour with prostitutes while his family lived on a very limited budget. Alwaki, in one of his many sermons, once denounced Zina, or fornication. He criticized American television for spreading Zina. Alwaki went so far as to say that Allah had sent AIDS to America as punishment.

Awlaki and his family would leave the U.S. and return to Yemen in 2002. In 2006-07 he spent 18 months in a Yemen prison on kidnapping charges. He was eventually released without trial and claimed he was arrested and held at the request of the U.S. government. This resentment and hatred of the American government would lead Awlaki to engage others in perpetrating violence here in the U.S. An example being communications between Awlaki and Army Major Nidal Hasan. Hasan, a U.S. Army Psychiatrist, went on a murderous rampage in November of 2009 killing 13 fellow soldiers at Fort Hood Army base in Texas. Hasan shouted "Allahu Akbar" (Arabic for "God is Great") as he emptied his semi-automatic pistol inside the processing center at Fort Hood.

Hasan, is a Virginia–born son of Palestinian immigrants. He graduated from Virginia Tech University and completed his psychiatry training at the Uniformed Services University of Health Services in Bethesda, Maryland, in 2003. He worked at Walter Reed Medical Center in Washington, D.C. treating soldiers returning from war with post-traumatic stress disorder. He was promoted to the rank of major in the Army in May of 2009 and was transferred to Fort Hood.

When reviewing the aftermath of his massacre, the Pentagon and a U.S. Senate committee found Hasan's superiors promoted him despite the fact that his behavior started to raise concerns. Behavior that suggested that Hasan had become radicalized and a potentially violent Islamic extremist. Reports show a carefully-planned plot by a lonely middle-aged man who apparently "self-radicalized" as he grew increasingly apart from colleagues over issues of politics and religion. Among Hasan's many rants, he stated that America's war on terror was, in fact, just a war on Islam. Some media reports state that Hasan tried to have some of his patients tried with war crimes after hearing their stories from the battlefield. The Army rebuffed all those charges. Still, what was the Army thinking? Was this not a huge red flag? Also, according to ABC News, while at Walter Reed Hasan once told a female superior that she'd be "ripped to shreds" because she was not a Muslim,. He stated to colleagues that Muslim soldiers should be released from service as conscientious objectors. Reports show that Walter Reed officials did not take actions against Hasan due to fears of a backlash for targeting a Muslim. Fort Hood officials say they had no knowledge of

Hasan's issues at Walter Reed. Business as usual, I guess. Pass the buck. Let's not offend anyone.

In 2013, Hasan, who was left paralyzed from the waist down by shots fired in trying to stop his carnage, was tried in military court. Hasan would choose to act as his own counsel. During his opening statement, he admitted he was the shooter. He stated that he was protecting both Muslims and Taliban leaders in Afghanistan by killing the soldiers at Fort Hood who were about to be deployed to that nation. During the course of the trial, Hasan called no witnesses and presented scant evidence. He also chose to give no closing argument. On August 23, 2013, Hasan was found guilty of 13 cases of premediated murder and 32 cases of attempted premeditated murder. He would be sentenced to death for his crimes. Hasan was also dismissed from the service, (nooo, really??) and sits in Fort Leavenworth, Kansas, awaiting execution while his case is reviewed by appellate courts.

Back to Awlaki. In 2010, he posted a video praising the actions of Major Hasan. He called the massacre a "heroic and wondrous act." Awlaki then went on to urge fellow Muslims to kill more American citizens in the name of Allah! Awlaki has also been tied to the failed plot to blow up a Detroit bound jetliner in Dec. 2009.

Nigerian Umar Farouk Abdulmutallab pled guilty in October 2011 in attempting to down the jetliner with a bomb sewn to his underwear. Yes, with a bomb sewn to his underwear! Administration officials at the time said Awlaki was the "mastermind" of the Christmas 2009 plot which could have killed 290 people if it was successful. A Justice Department memo states that Abdulmutallab stayed at the home of Awlaki while the attack was planned. Awlaki was also instrumental in writing the video "martyrdom" statement and that he introduced Abdulmutallab to the man who would design the explosive device to be used in the attempted bombing. I don't know about you, but I would have loved to have been at this meeting. "Ok Umar, we are going to attach a bomb to your underwear now...." " Not Awlaki's underwear, he's too important to have his private parts strewn all over Detroit, but you, Umar, you are the lucky jihadist to wear this very special package". (See what I did there?) Now I don't want to make light of this because if it had happened, it would have been a horrific event. But really, think how hard the task is in trying to prevent these acts from occurring? Especially when there are people actually willing to go to these lengths to perpetrate these crimes! Thankfully, the bomb didn't go off. It has been stated that Abdulmutallab wore the same underwear for two weeks straight. No lie. He traveled from Yemen to Africa and then the Netherlands before getting on a flight to Michigan. Abdulmutallab had hoped to have the bomb go off over the U.S. by injecting a syringe of chemicals into it, but thankfully, the chemicals only served to start a fire in Abdulmutallab's pants. No lie again. The fire was easily extinguished, and the attempted plot was thwarted. My favorite newspaper headline was the one in the New York Post, it read, "Great balls of Fire". Abdulmutallab pled guilty, and in Feb 2012 he was sentenced to life imprisonment without the possibility of parole. Abdulmutallab is currently incarcerated at the ADX Florence supermax prison near Florence, Colorado. Good riddance Umar bomb pants!

On October 29, 2010 two packages containing plastic explosives and a detonating device were found on separate cargo planes heading to the U.S. The bombs were found based on information given by Saudi Arabia's security chief. Both bombs were on flights that originated in Yemen. Thankfully, they were discovered when on scheduled in-route stopovers. One explosive was found on a stopover in the UK, the other found on a stopover in Dubai in the United Arab Emirates. A week later the AQAP, (al-Qaeda in the Arabian Peninsula), took credit for the plot. Both U.S. and British authorities believed Awlaki was also behind the plot. And get this, the bombs were believed to have been designed by one, Ibrahim Hassan al-Asiri, the genius behind the underwear bomb! The bombs were believed to be designed to explode midair with intentions of destroying both planes over Chicago or another city in the U.S.

The two packages used were actually Hewlett-Packard HP LaserJet P2055 desktop laser printers. Inside each printer's toner cartridge was a sophisticated bomb. They were filled with military-grade white powder plastic explosive. The explosive used was extremely hard to detect due to low vapor pressure. Whatever that is. It is evident that if we didn't receive the intelligence from Saudi Arabia, the explosives would not have been detected at checkpoints before taking off for the U.S. What was the goal of the AQAP? At worse, it would have given pause to world trade. UPS and FedEx would have probably gone bust. It could have been a full-blown disaster scenario.

On November 5, 2010, AQAP posted on several radical Islamist websites, "We will continue to strike blows against American interests and the interest of American allies...." "Since both operations were successful, we intend to spread the idea to our mujahedeen brothers in the world and enlarge the circle of its application to include civilian aircraft in the West as well as cargo aircraft."

AQAP also posted on November 21 a detailed account of the plot, including photos of the printer bombs in its English-language magazine run by Awlaki, Inspire. The article claimed the mission was a success because it caused a major disruption to the world's air traffic and security systems at the very low cost of $4200.

On November 2, four days after the bombs were discovered, Awlaki was charged in absentia in Yemen with plotting to kill foreigners and being an al-Qaeda member in an unrelated case. A Yemeni judge ordered Awlaki to be caught dead or alive.

One last example of the danger Awlaki posed is an incident involving an explosive device May 1, 2010, in Times Square in Manhattan, New York City. Two street vendors alerted security personnel after they spotted smoke coming from a vehicle. A car bomb was discovered. The bomb had been ignited, but it failed to explode and was dismantled without causing injuries. Two days later, federal agents arrested Faisal Shahzad, a

30-year-old Pakistan born resident of Bridgeport, Connecticut. Shahzad had become a U.S. citizen in April 2009. He was arrested as he boarded a flight to Dubai from JFK airport in New York. He admitted he was responsible for the failed car bombing and also told authorities that he trained at a Pakistani terror training camp. Shahzad also told interrogators that he was "inspired by" extremist Anwar al-Awlaki to take up the cause of al-Qaeda. He was motivated by Awlaki's writings calling for a holy war against the West as a religious duty, he was a big fan and follower of Awlaki. Shahzad made contact with Awlaki over the internet, as well as contact with other like-minded jihadists.

Shahzad had four other high profile targets in the New York area he wanted to hit if the first one was successful. On his list was Rockefeller Center, Grand Central Terminal, World Financial Center, (just across from Ground Zero) and a Connecticut-based company that makes helicopters for the U.S. military, Sikorsky. Shahzad showed the usual characteristics for an American jihadist. He felt Islam was under attack, and for a year prior to the attempted bombing, friends say Shahzad became more introverted, more religious, and more stringent in his views. Hiding in plain sight, being fed propaganda info from cunning Islamic extremist recruiters, ready to unleash mayhem and chaos on our country. Shahzad pled guilty to terror charges and on October 5, 2010, he was convicted and sentenced to life imprisonment without the possibility of parole. At his sentencing he stated, "...the demise of the U.S. is imminent." When asked by the judge, "Didn't you swear allegiance to this country?" Shahzad replied, "I sweared, but I didn't mean it." Fingers crossed perhaps? Goodbye failed bomber.

On September 30, 2011, two drones launched from a CIA base in Saudi Arabia fired Hellfire missiles at a vehicle carrying Anwar al-Awlaki. He was riding in the vehicle with three other suspected al-Qaeda operatives. All of the occupants were killed. At the time, President Obama spoke saying. "... Awlaki's death struck a blow to al-Qaeda in the Arabian Peninsula..." But the killing of Awlaki created a stir within the U.S. because

Awlaki was an American citizen, and his execution by the CIA was seen as violating his First Amendment protections of free speech and press. Really? It was also seen as violating his due process protections afforded him under the Constitution. The killing prompted debates that were both legal and moral in nature. Some see it as the ACLU does, (left) "...the U.S. targeted killing program is a program under which American citizens far from any battlefield can be executed by their own government without judicial process..." "...and on the basis of standards and evidence that are kept secret not just from the public but from the courts." Leading Republicans, like then Presidential candidate, Ron Paul, denounced Obama for "assassinating" al-Awlaki, saying that he should have been tried in a U.S. court.

U.S. Rep. Peter King, R-New York, who happened to be the chairman of the House Homeland Security Committee at the time, felt the strike was lawful. (right) He stated, "It was entirely legal. If a citizen takes up arms against his own country, he becomes an enemy of the country. The President was acting entirely within his rights, and I fully support the President."

U.S. authorities pointed to his involvement in the Fort Hood massacre, as well as his involvement in both the underwear bombing attempt and printer bombing attempt as proof to the danger Awlaki posed to American citizens. Being both an English speaker coupled with his facility with technology, Awlaki was seen as one of the top al-Qaeda recruiters in the world. Authorities considered him to be the face of the AQAP or al-Qaeda in the Arabian Peninsula.

Regardless on where you stand on this issue, the fact is that a very bad man was eliminated. But due to the wonders of the internet, however, his presence in the form of sermons recorded and papers written will live on and have a profound influence on future American jihadists.

Boston Marathon bomber Dzhokhar Tsarnaev was believed to have honed his hatred of Americans from the sermons recorded by Awlaki. His older brother, Tamerlan, who was killed by police in a shootout after the bombing, was also a disciple of Awlaki. Articles written by Awlaki were found downloaded to the younger Tsarnaev's computer, along with the first issue of *Inspire*, the webzine that Awlaki helped produce. In fact, officials linked the pipe bombs used by the Tsarnaev brothers in the Boston Marathon bombings to step-by-step instructions found in that first issue of *Inspire* webzine. Awlaki's influence was far reaching, way beyond the Tsarnaev brothers. According to the New America Foundation, since 9/11 there have been 52 American citizens or U.S. residents indicted in jihadists crimes or killed who have cited Awlaki as an influence. They either had in their possession his jihadist propaganda, met with him, or had some communication with him.

Side note, the New America Foundation is a non-partisan think tank that focuses on public policy issues such as national security, technology, health, gender, energy, education and the economy. It was founded in 1999 and is based in Washington. D.C. with offices in New York City as well. Its motto, "New America is committed to renewing American politics, prosperity, and purpose in the Digital Age." Ok? Thought you should know. Tough work, but I guess someone has to do it.

AQAP continues to publish *Inspire*. An issue published in March 2014 featured an interview with Awlaki right before his death. In it he urges for more attacks on Western civilians. Al-Qaeda and others motivated by extremist ideologies continue to view Awlaki as an important voice, so his sermons and writings will continue to appear on the internet. His influence will remain for future American jihadists. Scary thought indeed. There have been 16 issues of *Inspire* with the latest published in November 2016. When combing over the topics covered by the webzine, you find provocative topics such as the effectiveness of suicide bombings, the celebration of the Boston Marathon bombing, as well as the call for an increase of car bomb attacks in the U.S., and in one of its latest issues, strategies in converting black people in America to their cause. Whew. What can be done to combat this? If you shut down the site, his teachings will pop up on other sites. Perhaps Muslims leaders can step forward to denounce the teachings of Awlaki and *Inspire?* But to date that has been pretty much nonexistent.

There have been other horrific attacks here in the U.S. by Awlaki followers. On June 12 2016, in Orlando Florida, a self-radicalized jihadist by the name of Omar Mateen killed 49 people and wounded 53 others in a terrorist attack inside of a gay nightclub called Pulse. This incident holds several different distinctions. It was the deadliest mass shooting by a single shooter in United States history along with the deadliest incident of violence against LGBT people in U.S. history. Added to this is the fact that it was the deadliest terror attack here in the U.S. since the 9/11 attacks in 2001. Mateen was shot and killed by Orlando police after a three-hour standoff. A 9-1-1 call placed by Mateen while the attack was underway has Mateen swearing allegiance to the Islamic State of Iraq and Levant (ISIL) and stating the killings were tied to the U.S. killing of a fellow jihadist by the name of Abu Waheed in Iraq the previous month.

Mateen was a 29-year-old American born in New Hyde Park, New York. His parents were Afghan, and Mateen was raised a Muslim. At the time of his radicalization and subsequent killings, he resided in Fort Pierce, Florida. Ironically, Mateen unsuccessfully tried several times to enter into a law enforcement career. Once as a prison guard for the Florida Department of Corrections and later he attempted to become a Florida State Trooper and gain admission into a police academy. The warden recommended administrative termination based on a claim that Mateen joked about bringing a gun to the school. In 2007, a classmate of Mateen at the police academy claimed he threatened to shoot fellow recruits at a cookout "after his hamburger touched pork."

Since 2007, Mateen was employed as a security guard and had an active statewide firearms license and an active security guard license. He also passed a psychological test and had no prior criminal background. His psychological test was called into question when the psychologist listed denied ever interviewing Mateen, and not living in Florida at the time the test was administered. The company that hired Mateen, G4S Secure Solutions, stated that a "clerical error" on his form led to the wrong psychologist being named. The correct Doctor claimed he never interviewed Mateen, but instead analyzed a standard test that Mateen took before being hired. Oppps. G4S was later fined for their lapses in administering psychological testing to new hires. Small consolation indeed.

Mateen was married twice. His first wife claimed Mateen was physically abusive and that he was a regular steroid user. Mateen's autopsy indicated that he was in fact, a habitual steroid abuser. His ex-wife also claimed that she believed Mateen was "mentally unstable" and "mentally ill." This from a lay-person, not a psychologist! He was married to his second wife at the time of the shootings and had a young son.

Mateen was a walking, talking contradiction. While he stated to co-workers his hatred of "black people, women, Jews, Hispanics and gay and lesbian people" (That's a lot of hatred to hold in one's heart.), there were several instances where Mateen was believed to have had homosexual encounters. The first was with a fellow male classmate who stated that Mateen once asked him on a date and that they had spent time at gay bars after work. Another instance was with a man who identified himself as Mateen's lover of two-months. That man believes the killings might have been carried out for revenge. He stated that Mateen believed a Hispanic man may have given him HIV after a sexual encounter. His autopsy indicated he was not HIV infected. Several patrons of Pulse, the nightclub Mateen shot up, stated that they had seen him at the club many times before the massacre. He allegedly used several different gay dating apps to solicited dates with men. With all this being reported, the FBI had their doubts about Mateen being gay. They say they found no text-messages, cellphone apps, or cell tower location information leading them to believe he had any type of homosexual lifestyle, closeted or otherwise.

The question is: Was this an act of terrorism or a horrific hate crime? Some would argue that Mateen had a lethal combination of self-radicalization coupled with a healthy dose of deep seeded self-hatred. His ties to Islamic jihadists is unquestioned. Connections to both Awlaki and his videos along with alleged ties to other jihadists prompted the FBI in 2013 to put Mateen under surveillance. Although Mateen was followed, interviewed by undercover informants, and had his communications and spending monitored, the FBI chose to close the investigation, deemed to not pose a credible threat. Mateen was a complicated man, driven by self-loathing, homophobia and jihadism. When conferring with the experts, you don't get a consensus on what was the real motivation behind the massacre.

As one can see, the problems surrounding self-radicalized jihadists are many. So what's the answer to identifying and redirecting potential jihadists in our country? How do you combat this rhetoric?

> *"Islam was never a religion of peace. Islam is the religion of fighting. No one should believe that the war that we are waging is the war of the Islamic State. It is the war of all Muslims, but the Islamic state is spearheading it. It is the war of Muslims against infidels."*
>
> —ABU BAKR AL-BAGHDADI
> (ISIS LEADER AND SELF-PROCLAIMED EMIR OF THE CALIPHATE)

Or this gem from Abu Mohammed al-Adnani (ISIS spokesman)

> ..."*Kill any disbeliever, whether he be French, American, or any of their allies.*"

The FBI reports that it has more than 900 active investigations of alleged ISIS sympathizers throughout our 50 states. The experts are divided on the methods that should be used to eradicate domestic terrorism. Some believe that by going "over there" to destroy ISIS, we will solve our threat of homegrown terrorism. Others would argue that by doing so we are only inflaming the passions and increasing the threat of domestic violence and feeding into the propaganda of the U.S. killing innocent Muslims around the world. Still others believe it might be impossible to destroy the ideology of violent jihadism.

Diplomat and Middle East expert, Chas Freeman, explains that by using military power you "...radicalize and create voluntary recruits for our own worst enemies." He believes that "we need to halt military strikes not double down on them."

Daniel L. Davis, a highly decorated retired Lt. Col. In the U.S. Army who served 4 combat deployments and recently retired after 21-year career, has a very similar approach. He highlights five points:

1. Suspend politics based on the belief that the U.S. can impose a set of values and a political system of our own preference on others alien to it.

2. Do all we can diplomatically, politically, and economically to contain the fire of Islamic radicalism to where it now burns.

3. Work with allies to help stop the spread by choking off funds, interdicting resupply chains, and blocking routes by which new radicals join the fight.

4. Stop bombing terror targets from the air. This will be the hardest and most controversial step because it seems counterintuitive to suggest that to best battle terrorism is to stop bombing them. But overwhelming evidence, according to Davis, confirms that such tactics work against our interests.

5. Use the military to contain ISIS where it exists now, then employ new diplomatic measures that have a chance to undermine the terrorists.

Hmm. A little hard to digest? Remember this is from a military hero who has had boots on the ground and has studied the situation for many years.

Humera Khan, Executive Director of the anti-terrorism Think Tank, Muflehun, and advisor to several government agencies including the FBI, has a plan to battle self-radicalizing jihadists here in the U.S. She believes the key is to raise awareness. Awareness in the community, schools, and at home. Awareness from the professionals who deal with our youth, as well as providing awareness for the parents. Get to the kids before they start the radicalization process. Dissuade them from joining in the first place. If not caught in the prevention phase and have started to go down the path to radicalization, there is a great need for intervention. Examples are engaging Imams to provide counseling. Other forms of prevention can be carried out in community centers.

Intervention works best when provided as early as possible. Hire mentors and youth center directors to reach out to the vulnerable youth. They will be able to detect, along with family, any changes in behavior or opinions. Deal with it before ideals set, making it a whole lot harder to deconstruct them. Another important weapon is to use social media. It is effectively used by Islamic recruiters, so why not use it as an intervention to pull people back.

Some background on Muflehun. It is an independent non-profit "…at the nexus of society, security, and technology, working since 2010 against hate, extremism and violence." This was taken directly from their website. "Muflehun" means, "those who have cultivated their success/prosperity." Whatever that is. They provide community-led early intervention services to support families concerned about loved ones being recruited towards any potentially violent activity. To maintain their independence, they rely on the goodness of your heart, but more importantly your pocketbook. This is not a government agency, and some have called this organization the 'glue" between national and local organizations. Muflehun refuses funding from the U.S. Dept. of Defense, Dept. of Homeland Security or any other security based government agency. It also refuses support from any foreign government. Hence, the independent status.

When looking at solutions and approaches to domestic terrorism, I found several entities offering help. One is something called Viral Peace. They believe in resilience building to prevent hate, extremism and violence. Their workshops are geared to youth activists or what they call change-makers. They provide strategies to push back the forces behind the hate, extremism, and violence that could potentially influence our youth. They use social media to build their own narrative. They want to stand up to the negative propaganda spewing from the Islamic recruiters. This organization can be found in over ten different countries.

Another such organization is called Rampoff. They are an information and early intervention support service. They help family members and peers identify early behavior signs which could lead to extremist views and/ or behaviors. They provide what is lacking in the communities in terms of understanding the potential problems. They also compensate for the lack of support services within the communities they serve. Rampoff sees itself as an alternative for concerned citizens to get needed help without law enforcement involvement. They guide citizens to long-term support services within their communities.

An organization that I'm sure we all aware of is Google. In 2015 Google restructured and created a public holding company known as Alphabet Inc. Google is one of many different companies to exist under the Alphabet Inc. umbrella. Another subsidiary created within Alphabet Inc. is something called Jigsaw, formerly known as Google Ideas. You following? Within Jigsaw is a project called the Redirect Method. Whew. A long-winded route to the crux of the matter. Redirect uses the Google AdWords platform along with YouTube to target prospective ISIS recruits and attempt to dissuade them from joining the group. Redirect uses interviews with ISIS defectors and jailed recruits and places them alongside results for any keywords and phrases that are used when searching anything related to ISIS. They also link to Arabic-English language YouTube channels that contain videos which Jigsaw believes can undo ISIS's brainwashing.

Included are testimonials from defectors, former extremists, and Imams denouncing ISIS's corruption of the religion of Islam. They also include clips from inside the dysfunctional caliphate in both Northern Syria and Iraq.

Does it work? Google claims that during a pilot program conducted in 2016, advertising was 3 to 4 times more effective than for an ordinary campaign. They say that, "…those who clicked spent more than twice as long viewing the most effective playlists than the best estimates of how people view YouTube as a whole."

Yasmin Green, Jigsaw's head of research and development, states, "The Redirect Method is at its heart a targeted advertising campaign: Let's take these individuals who are vulnerable to ISIS' recruitment messaging and instead show them information that refutes it."

There are some who think the most effective way to utilize Jigsaw would be to target would-be ISIS recruits identified by use of keywords for surveillance and possibly arrests instead. The feeling is that intercepting ISIS sympathizers would not only rescue those recruits themselves, but also potential victims of terrorist violence. The company, to its credit, has handed over 64% of the more than 40,000 government requests for its user data in just a six-month period. But the company maintains that the Redirect Method is in place to educate not surveil or arrest users. They want to arm people with more and better information in regard to ISIS and its recruitment propaganda.

Well, there you have it, Jihadism in America. It is both complicated and dangerous. There are some very bad people trying to recruit within our country and perpetuate violent acts. This needs both vigilance and resources to combat. It will take many different levels of involvement, from the family to the U.S. government, along with community programs and schools. But we all agree, it has to get done!

CHAPTER TWO

Has Anybody Seen
the Middle-Class?

B efore examining the current state of the economy here in the U.S., let's first look back at the economy coming into this century. Some economists have claimed that the U.S. economy entering the 21st century was bigger and more successful than ever. In the first half of the previous century, the U.S. economy survived two World Wars and a devastating global depression. It then proceeded to go head to head with the Soviets in a costly 40-year Cold War and emerge victorious. The economy survived extended periods of sharp inflation, high unemployment, and monstrous government budget deficits. But the 1990's gave the U.S. a period of economic calm. Prices finally stabilized, and unemployment figures were at its lowest in 30 years. The Clinton administration actually produced a budget surplus! Something that has not been seen since. By the end of the century, the stock market had hit unprecedented levels.

Another indicator of our economic health at the end of the 20th century was America's gross domestic product – the total output of goods and services. Late 1990's saw our GDP exceeding $8.5 trillion. That's trillion with a T! To frame it another way, although the U.S. accounts for less than 5% of the world's population, it accounts for over 25% of the world's total economic output. The second largest economy, Japan, is approximately half the size of America's economy. The American economy thrived in the 1990's while the rest of the world's economies showed slowed growth and other economic problems. In fact, the U.S. experienced the longest period of uninterrupted expansion in its history during the 1990's!

But there were also indications of problems ahead. Innovations in computing, telecommunications, and sciences were affecting how Americans both worked and played. The world around us was changing. The collapse of the Soviet Union, re-emergence of Western Europe, growing strength of Latin America, and the globalization of business and finance presented both opportunities and risks. Many workers at the end of the 20th century looked toward the future with plenty of uncertainty.

Long-term challenges lurked. While the economy was indeed humming along, there were also large segments of the population living in poverty. A larger gap developed between the rich and poor. The number of people without proper healthcare grew, all this while living in a very affluent United States. There were also problems attached to the aging baby-boomer generation. The boomers were approaching retirement age as we headed towards the 21st century, a situation that would tax both our nation's pension and health-care systems.

Other problems surfaced at the end of the 20th century such as the disappearance of our manufacturing sector, along with unsurmountable trade deficits with other countries. But our country stuck to its core values and its belief in the "free enterprise system." We remained a "market economy," which is an economy that works best when decisions about what to produce, and at what price to sell, are left to individual buyers and sellers. Ideally this is an economy void of governmental or powerful private intervention. Yeah, right. These values also extended itself into our political realm as well. During the 20th century, government leaders opened up many industries to private competition. Changes were seen in the airline, banking, telephone, and utility industries. The decades of the '70s, '80s, and '90s all saw deregulations that once sheltered these industries from market competition. The government put legislation in place to open up our economy to more competition.

While the size of our government grew from the 1930's (Great Depression) to the 1970's, which made many weary about an over-reaching governmental presence, the 1980's (Reagan era) we saw the size of our government decline. Major social programs like Social Security and Medicare, which provides retirement income and healthcare for the elderly, managed to survive during this tumultuous period.

As we entered the 21st century, debates over deregulation of industries, government spending, and welfare reform took center stage. What is the proper role for our government in our economy? Incidentally, this is a debate that has waged for over 200 years, ever since the United States became an independent nation. As more things change, the more they stay the same.

Let's turn our focus to the economy of the 21st century. We experienced slow economic growth during the beginning of the 21st century. The national debt is said to be our problem. This debt is said to be stifling our growth. Not just the U.S. government, but individuals, and private companies, are all borrowing. All this borrowing gives the illusion of economic growth, but that game is coming to an end. While the U.S. struggles to pay down debt, balance the budget, and fund investments for our future, many families are also struggling with debt, bills, and bleak futures. To many, it seems an unsurmountable task. How do you get ahead while paying for the past and the present? Many economists feel that if our economy continues to grow at a mere 1-2% rate per year, our economic future is grim indeed.

The future of families are also bleak as well, with raises of 1-2% per year. Raises? Did I just say raises? 1-2% per year? Many are just thankful for jobs. Raises? But let's set our focus on the U.S. economy first, then I'll bring it back to the family or individual level. Macro-economics, then micro-economics.

On the macro level, economic experts feel that if we can raise the growth rate to 4-5%, we would be able to easily balance the budget. Along with that, we would be able to pay down current debt and invest in our future. We could improve our infrastructure, lower unemployment, raise the standard of living, and fund a strong military to protect our interests. What's the problem then? Many say it's politics. And within this world of politics we have two warring factions. These factions are better known as the Democratic and Republican parties. And according to the experts, (whoever they are?) neither party knows what the hell its doing when dealing with our economy. The economic experts feel politicians must stop with the sound bites. They must put their best thinking forward, along with good old hard work. Then we might have a better chance to build and sustain a high growth economy. That's much easier said than done. It would require some original thinking and sacrifice. Two things that seem to be in short supply today in the political world.

So, what is the solution? How do we grow this economy and make it work for everyone? And more importantly, why should we care? Well, a growing economy puts more money into families' pockets. It also puts more of the unemployed back to work. And believe it or not, it could increase your nest egg for your children's education, or… wait for it….your much deserved retirement! Here are some myths, passed off as sound economic policies, spewed by our inept public officials. Why myths, you ask? Because many economists feel it is based on fairy tales rather than reality. Don't fall for the MYTH!

- **Myth #1: Government spending grows the economy by pumping money into it!**

Well, look at this logically. Where is the government getting the money that it will pump into the economy? It is either taxed or borrowed from individuals, businesses or even other countries. This doesn't increase production or create wealth. All this does is move money around from within the economy. So this does not encourage economic growth or increase the family bank account. Borrowing from Peter to pay Paul does not grow an economy. There is no new income growth, just a redistribution of income. The idea that the government pumping money into the economy making it grow is ill-advised at best. Fairy tale.

- **Myth #2: Government spending makes people more productive!**

Really? Again, let's use simple logic here, folks. Let's face it, when are we more productive; when things are handed to us or when we have to work for them? Critics say Welfare programs that are now in place in the U.S. only encourages recipients to rely on government handouts rather than go to work. The programs that work best, therefore, are those programs designed to get people back to work. Workfare rather than welfare. Multiple results follow. You increase the new worker's dignity and decrease their dependence on government handouts. You can also reduce the opposition who feel taken advantage of by the system. Mostly the average worker who feels that their hard-earned money is being diverted to those who choose to sit on their asses and collect a government check. When more people are at work, productivity tends to rise, and an economy tends to grow. Period, end of sentence!

Some feel government programs discourage good economic choices. Programs such as Social Security and Medicare that cover retirement, and low-income housing tax-credits that cover housing. These programs are said to discourage savings by individuals. (Savings, what's savings?). You can throw in Pell Grants used for higher education as well. The thinking here is, why should people put aside money for these high expenses if they can expect the government to be there for them when they need it?

We have to weigh the real costs to these government controlled programs against their real, not imagined or promised, benefits. With that said, the government should instead focus its attention on specific things that could actually improve many people's productivity. The most popular example used in today's economic discussions is the improvement of our country's infrastructure. This has a two-fold rippling effect with our economy. It can reduce transportation costs along with increasing productivity within the transportation sector. This productivity will be felt throughout the rest of our economy. Another idea is to increase government spending on long-term research. Think the space program from prior times. These projects increase incomes and productivity in the long-term. But that's the rub. Research can be costly and highly uncertain (Can we actually land someone on the moon and get them back?) and research usually shows returns many years after the initial investment. Can our government show the resolve needed for such an investment? We would need creative and forward thinking here folks.

- **Myth #3: The Federal government should bail out faltering industries and States to revive the economy!**

Bailouts actually harm an economy. It rewards reckless private as well as state spending. It leaves such actions unchecked and only encourages the behaviors in the future. Again, the government will be there for us no matter what reckless decisions we make. A very smart man was once quoted over 2500 years ago as saying:

"If you want to encourage something, reward it. If you want to discourage it, punish it." Aristotle was the smart guy's name, and he might have been on to something, huh? Bailout money comes from taxpayers. When President Obama bailed out the automotive and then the banking industries in our last economic crisis of 2008, it was met with mixed reviews to say the least. There were some who felt that if you want to stimulate the economy, help the consumers, not the corporations. Don't bail out failed industries, instead put that money into the hands of the consumers who would then put it back into the economy. Pay off or at least pay down people's mortgages was an idea thrown out there. Nice idea, but not feasible. The crisis of 2008 was bigger than a mortgage crisis, and it needed swift immediate attention. To stave off the threat of another Great Depression, these industries needed help and help now. It saved tens of thousands of jobs and averted a far larger catastrophic financial crisis.

The same can be said about failing states. When the federal government bails out these states, they are effectively taking money from all citizens. The states that have acted responsibly get no reward. The state that acted recklessly does. This only encourages the responsible state to act more recklessly in the future, knowing that big brother will be there when they need him. Many feel that Congress should resist these state bailouts and have state governments set priorities, make trade-offs, and reduce unnecessary spending. Those states taking part in deficit spending should not demand from the federal government money from the more responsible states.

- **Myth #4: Public works projects jumpstarts an economy by creating new jobs!**

Hmm…no, it doesn't says some experts. In the short-term, they say it does not have any real effect on employment. It serves to take money away from the private sector and move workers to the government payroll or to place the burden once again on the taxpayers. Another negative of public works projects is the need for extensive bureaucracy and red tape. Two very bad words when dealing with efficiency and competency. Throw in a lack of accountability and lack of motivation for the efficient use of taxpayers' money, and you have a recipe for disaster. This blocks economic growth, which centers on productivity.

- **Myth #5: Tax cuts only serve to fatten the pockets of the rich and does nothing to help a weakened economy!**

Experts argue that an economy will grow when taxes are cut and more money is in people's pockets. Higher taxes with higher government spending is counter-productive to a growing economy. All it manages to do is divert money from one sector to another within the economy. Experts see fault with the United States progressive income tax system as well. In a progressive income tax system, your income is taxed at a higher rate as your income rises. Your last dollar earned is taxed higher than your first dollar earned. Critics claim that a progressive tax damages incentives to a growing economy. Incentives such as more hours worked, more money saved, and more dollars invested. For an economy to grow, businesses need to produce increasing amounts of existing goods and services, while also creating new products and services. In order to do this, you need investment capital for new technologies and facilities, along with a motivated workforce. The higher tax rates on the last dollars earned hinder economic growth because they are the dollars which are usually allocated to savings and investing. Most people take care of necessities first, then save and invest as they earn more. The same goes for small businesses and large corporations. Progressive taxation hinders this effort. Economists feel that a proportional tax system (or flat-tax system) would be best in growing an economy. Everyone pays at the same tax rate. The more you earn, the more you pay. But everyone pays at the same, not increasing, tax rate. For example, with a 10% proportional tax rate, someone making $40,000 per year would pay $4000. Someone making $80,000 would pay $8000. Under the current progressive system, the person making $80,000 would pay $16,000, in effect, a 20% rate. Taxing your last dollars earned at a higher rate. This curtails the saving and investing needed to grow an economy.

Overall tax cuts works. History bears this out. There were significant tax cuts in the decades of the 1920's, 1960's and 1980's. All three decades saw increased investment and robust economic growth followed. Unfortunately our lawmakers tend to balk at reducing the tax rate and seldom restrain from over spending. Government policies have a huge effect on a growing economy. But as you see, moving money from one sector to another doesn't do the trick. These policies are based on "myths" not reality. In fact, these "myths" do more harm than good to an economy. Only when lawmakers put into effect reality-based programs will we see our economy grow once more.

Now on to the micro-economic level. What's going on with our pocketbooks? What has happened and what can we expect? As we headed into the 21st century, we were experiencing a an uptick in terms of wages and the number of people at work in America. The year 2000 saw the overall unemployment rate at a low not seen since 1969. The overall rate was at 4%. The rates for blacks and Hispanics were at lows that were never seen (7.6% for blacks, 5.7% for Hispanics). But when a recession hit us in 2001, the unemployment rate inched up to a high of 6% in 2003, and after the great recession of 2008, unemployment hit an overall high of 10% in October 2010. That's more than double the rate as we entered the century. I'm glad to say that the unemployment rate has since dropped back to 4.5% as of March 2017. But what a rollercoaster ride it has been.

What about the working class in America? You know, the everyday people who get up early and put in a hard day's work. How is life going for them? Are they living better today than in the past? Well the short answer folks is no. Life for the working people in America has been a struggle. You hear a lot about the shrinking middle class. Is this so? What does that really mean? The things that go along with a middle-class lifestyle is now out of reach for many working families. We are talking about things such as cars, homes, educations for kids, and basic healthcare for the families. For those families who do purchase these items, chances are they are going into massive debt to achieve it. Let's look at some numbers to bring this into perspective. I will compare items as they cost in 1975 (adjusted to 2015 dollars) to what they cost at the end of 2015. These are median prices from throughout the 50 states:

Good or service	1975 cost (adjusted to $2015)	2015 cost	% Inc/Dec
New house	$209,417	$270,200	+29%
New car	$16,578	$31,252	+47%
Public college	$7,938	$18,943	+150%
Private college	$16,475	$42,419	+160%
Healthcare (2004)	$4,550	$9,300	+104%
Median income	$55,374	$51,759	-6.5%
Minimum wage	$9.16	$8.25	-9.9%

This chart shows how items such as homes, cars, college, and healthcare, have risen dramatically over time, while income and the minimum wage have declined in real dollars. When people wonder why it's more difficult in today's world financially, no need to look any further! The median U.S. household today is actually poorer than it was in 1975. There's not enough money for the working class people to spend on the things necessary to carry out a traditional middle-class lifestyle. So the blame game begins. Who does the finger get pointed towards? Well, in 2012 a Pew Research Survey of over 1,200 self-described middle-class families, they blamed the following: 62% blamed Congress; 54% blamed banks and other financial institutions; 47% large corporations; 44% the Bush Administration; 39% foreign competition; 34% the Obama Administration; and 8% blamed the middle class itself. On top of that, a whopping 85% said it was much harder now than a decade earlier to maintain their standard of living. It gives me little comfort to know I am not alone in this. Almost 9 out of 10 American families feel the same strain as my family does. You want more stats you say? Well, how about this one! The middle class tier in 1971 was over 61% of all adults. Today? That figure shrinks to under 50%. 10% of the so-called middle class has vanished. Wow. One last one. When talking about the total household pie in the U.S., the upper class takes 46% (up from 29% in the 1970's), middle class 45% (down from 61%) and lower class takes in 9% (down from 10%). Again, the middle class hit hardest.

Now let's get into the whole wealth disparity scenario while we are at it, shall we? The top 1% of our economy controls 42% of all the wealth in

America. Well ok, that still leaves 58% of the wealth for the rest of the 99% of the people, right? Well actually, no. On further examination, you see that the top 10% of our economy controls 93% of the wealth, so the remaining 90% of the people have a meager 7% to fight over. My head is about to explode from all these numbers. What it boils down to is this: Not since the Great Depression have we seen such lopsided data. The rich are definitely getting richer while the rest of us are fighting over the scraps. That's the New American reality. Oh, and by the way, the bottom 90% has 73.5% of all U.S. debt, while the top 10% has 26.5% of all U.S. debt. Yay, we win at something! It's a bleak picture indeed.

What can be done to bring back the middle class? One solution heard many times is to shift some of the tax burden from the middle class to the upper class. Tax the rich more. In its simplicity, it seems appealing, at least for those of us who identify ourselves as not rich. When you take a look at the source of a family's income, it usually comes in two forms. First is the market wages earned. Second is the government transfers received by that family. Basically, your job and the government programs that are put in place to help you. A government transfer is a one-way payment made by the government to an individual or family without a transfer of money, goods, or services back to the government. Cynics would call this a handout. Usually, rich cynics. Most would call this needed relief for a family or person in order to survive. Examples of government transfer programs are: social security; old-age or disability pensions; student grants; unemployment compensation; etc. Non-cynics would call this a safety net. Something all of us (those in the working class at least) have probably depended on sometime in our lives. Relieving some of the tax burden from the middle-class and placing it on the higher tax brackets will certainly help out. But will it happen?

Another popular solution to help working families is to expand the Earned Income Tax Credit. This would serve to put more money in the hands of families who could use it most. But it is only a short-term solution. The underlying problem that needs to be addressed is how to increase worker productivity in order to grow our economy. How can we get the U.S. economic growth rate up to 4-5% as we talked about earlier? I cringe when I hear people say that we need to increase workers' productivity because the people I know are working their butts off. They are barely holding their heads above water. We are also talking both husband and wife working full-time jobs. It's like running on a treadmill, working hard and going nowhere fast. Sweating your butt off and ending up in the same place. Get the picture yet?

Some politicians have advocated for just the opposite. They call for a reduction of government spending on these safety-net programs. Too much government support they crow, is just a disincentive to work. They talk about the loosening of eligibility requirements for programs such as Social-Security Disability Insurance as one of the reasons for a decline in the numbers of working men. They go on to say that the so-called safety-net programs in place have actually hurt the very people it intends to help. Really, Richey Rich? So say the men with corporate bonuses and golden parachutes at retirement, the people with trust fund money and generations of wealth to provide a safety net.

Rich countries are rich enough to help its citizens live decent lives. Living well doesn't mean to work as many hours as possible to raise productivity. It takes a combination of productive worker participation and also government protections in place for cases such as poverty and sickness. Not all of us have daddy's money to fall back on, Richey Rich. The programs put in place by our government are an essential factor to a safe and productive working class.

Another possible solution is maybe we should concentrate our efforts not on reorganizing the government but instead, reorganize workers. The Golden Age for the middle class was the 1960's, no doubt. Coincidentally this period was also the height of union membership in our workforce. Well, then, let's get unionized and return to this Golden Age! If only it was that simple. Nothing about this is simple. It is a fact that both union membership and the share of income by the middle class are both in a decline since the 1960's. But is this decline in income actually a result of a decline in union membership? Does one have to do with the other? Maybe technology and globalization has a part to play in this as well? Perhaps an even bigger part to play. Demand for unskilled workers are in decline as we automate and globalize our manufacturing industries. The current job market requires a more skilled and diverse workforce. Many in this diverse workforce seem disinterested in tying their economic outcomes to the other workers among them. There is nothing to bind these workers, unlike the homogenous workers of the 20th century. Many of these multi-national corporations operate and employ around the globe. It's tough enough to get people from one close geographic area to unionize, try to get people from the U.S., Bombay, and Taiwan to band together. The 21st century has seen the enormous growth of the internet providing many low-cost products. Think Walmart and think Amazon. If the 20th century was the time for workers, the 21st century might be the time for consumers. And those consumers might not be so inclined to pay the higher prices that comes from more expensive labor.

If the 21st century is all about globalism, maybe we should go ahead and try to protect what we have here. Perhaps a bit of protectionism. Keep what's ours, right here in the good ole' US of A. The most popular suggestion here is to repeal NAFTA. Many point to NAFTA as one of the reasons behind stagnant wages and loss of jobs. The global market that has been created, has hurt the American worker and especially the middle class. Other experts point to the fact that at most, 350,000 jobs have been lost due to NAFTA. Although that is a big thing to 350,000 workers and their families, it only accounts for 0.25 percent of the labor force, therefore, not a determining factor in the downsizing of our middle class. So what does that leave us with?

What we need to do is to change the mindset of both workers and government officials. Instead of thinking that economic growth will lead to a burgeoning middle class, let's think instead that the middle class is the source of the economic growth. Economic growth doesn't lead to a growing middle class; it's the middle class that leads to economic growth. Subtle, but a profound change in thinking. With a stronger middle class, you have a stronger, more stable consumer base. When this base gains more economic power, productivity will rise to meet the demand. When you reawaken this sleeping giant other benefits are seen as well. You would see a growing desire for entrepreneurship and innovation. Both of these benefits also lead to a rise in economic growth. This isn't new thinking here, folks. John Maynard Keynes, renowned British economist, in his 1936 book, *The General theory of Employment, Interest and Money,* wrote about the ties of the middle class to economic growth. He wrote back then that stable middle-class consumption is the key to further investments within an economy. Keynes and other influential economists talk of core mechanisms leading to middle-class led growth. Factors such as stable demand, trust and good governance, and forward-thinking capitalistic policies.

The only way to entice new investments within an economy is to have sufficient consumption of current inventory. Raising the levels of current consumption will motivate private investors to get involved in the economy. The end result is the growth of an economy. Buy up what's available so that investors are motivated to pour more money into the economy and spur economic growth. All is good and dandy. What has happened in today's world is that many who set policies have forgotten a very important point made by Keynes in this regard. The importance Keynes placed on the middle class in creating sufficient demand to stimulate growth. Keynes argued that what we see in today's economy, the uneven distribution of income, only decreases demand and slows economic growth. As rich as the rich are, they simply don't consume enough to drive an economy. The wealthy tend to save more and consume less. I guess that's why their wealthy, huh? So, when wages are stagnant or declining, there isn't enough demand to encourage productive investment. Unless of course, demand becomes debt fueled. But as we all should know by now, this type of consumption never lasts forever. Eventually, credit stops flowing, and we see deep recessions that take years for us to recover from. This slows growth for long periods of time. The picture becomes clearer: The middle class needs to be able to consume products to have economic growth, and the way to do that is to raise the middle class incomes. I'm all in on this. How about you? Raise wages and reduce the tax burden on the middle-class will serve to stimulate consumption, thereby increasing investment which leads to economic growth! Seems pretty clear to me.

The next point is more common sense. If people are doing better financially, they tend to become more trusting. They are more optimistic and start to believe they can control their own circumstances. When you have these conditions, people tend to work together in both business and life. People are less grouchy when they have a few more bucks in their pockets. At least I know I am. With higher levels of trust, you will see that people are willing to innovate and take more sound economic risks. Working together instead of looking over their shoulders, wondering who is after their jobs. Can't we all just get along goes a long way to economic growth, or so it seems.

This leads to the next point. With a more contented middle class, you should see a better run government, mainly because people will feel more motivated to participate in the electoral process. People would feel that they now have a stake in the government and its policies. Higher participation levels mean the concerns of the middle class will not be ignored. This would also reduce factional politics and start to promote policies that benefit all levels of society instead of benefitting only those at the top. But this seems to me to be just pie-in-the-sky thinking. Sounds nice, but can it ever happen? Working people don't need utopian pipedreams to be spouted. Working people need concrete advances.

One concrete way to improve the earning and buying power of the middle class is to increase overtime pay. Overtime for the middle class has virtually disappeared. In 1975, more than 65 percent of salaried employees earned time-and-a-half pay for every hour worked over 40 hours per week. This was not out of any generosity by the capitalist back then, it was the law! Here's the thing, it's still the law. But the salary level at which employers are required to pay overtime has dramatically eroded over time. In fact, it is below the poverty level for a family of four. So, in other words, in order to qualify for overtime today, you have to earn below poverty level income. Wow. In real dollars that equates to $ 23,660 per year or lower to qualify for mandatory overtime. In 2013, only 11% of all workers qualified for mandatory overtime. Absorb that for a moment, 1975- 65%, 2013-11%. And employers have been working the remaining 89% harder, with unlimited hours and no overtime pay. Working people are working longer than ever, making less money than ever, with prices soaring for the basic goods needed to provide for your family. I'm pissed just writing this.

To get back to the 1975 levels of workers getting overtime, (65% of workers), the threshold for overtime would have to be raised to $69,000. Anyone making less would qualify for overtime pay. This increase would affect over 10 million workers in our economy. Either workers would be paid more or they would at least have more time with their families. And if employers don't want to pay the overtime to their workers, in order to maintain production levels, additional workers would have to be hired. Unemployment would decrease and wages would be driven upward.

The President has the power to do this without prior congressional approval. And the President could even go further if so inclined or at least if he is interested in getting the middle class back on its feet. He could change the rules for those who are currently exempt from overtime, professions such as teachers, federal employees, doctors, computer professionals and the like. And by the way, corporate leaders are lobbying hard to expand "computer professional" to mean just about anybody who uses a computer.

Which is just about everybody! By narrowing these exemptions, millions more would feel the benefits. The question should not be "why should those workers earn overtime", it should be "why not?" How did we come to this point of denying overtime to workers? Having people work longer hours with no extra pay? There is no other explanation than that it benefits the corporate elite, the group of people who have seen astronomical gains in their incomes while the vast majority of workers have seen none.

The biggest obstacle is the thinking that it would wreak havoc on a corporation's bottom line. It would force a corporation to lay off workers. This thinking is old trickle-down economics. Workers earning more would be bad for business and the economy. Well let's go to the scorecard please. In the good old days for the middle class, (1950-1980), corporate profits averaged a healthy 6% of GDP. Since 1980 that percentage has doubled to a whopping 12% of GDP. Translated into real dollars, that means corporations have gained an average of a TRILLION dollars per YEAR. To add more misery to the workers, wages have fallen by the same 6% of GDP. Coincidence? Don't fall for it. Profits have risen for no other reason than that it was allowed to. The rise in profits could just easily have been shared with the workers in the form of wage increases or the consumers in terms of discounts. But it also comes down to bargaining leverage; the rich have it, and workers don't.

I would venture a guess that most middle-class workers don't even realize they are being ripped off. Most business owners don't even keep track of your hours. They give you a job and trust you to do it in the time allotted. But the fact is you get handed twice as much work as you can reasonably do in a 40-hour work week. This forces people to work harder, longer. This also enables the employers to limit the number of workers needed to get the job done. Unemployment numbers rise, and as the unemployment figure rises, it is used to "motivate" workers to "do what it takes" to keep your job. So, workers work harder, longer, pushing unemployment up and wages down. And look no further, this is what keeps workers poor, and corporations rich.

According to a recent Gallup poll, salaried employees in America now report working an average of 47 hours per week. The same poll shows that 18 percent of salaried employees work over 60 hours per week. At the same time, these workers are only taking 77% of their paid time off. American workers average 16 vacation days out of the 21 them are allotted. This is the lowest total seen in the last 40 years. And the answer given most by the workers when asked why this is, they are afraid of falling short of their employer's demands for more productivity. Here's a fact, the forfeited vacation time adds up to an estimated $52 billion that goes straight to the owners. Another win for them.

Pushing up the overtime threshold for salaried employees is the same as raising the minimum wage for the poor. The minimum wage has eroded from an inflation-adjusted peak of $11 an hour in 1968 to only $7.25 today. By raising the minimum wage, you would also see a rise in wages for those slightly above the minimum. If you raise the threshold to $69,000 to qualify for overtime, you would see a general rise in wages for those above the threshold as well. Sounds too good to ever happen. Capitalists would tell you that cutting into corporate profits would dramatically impair the economy. What would happen to all the great investments made by the capitalists, investments such as creating more good-paying jobs for Middle America? Yeah, right. The only investments being made from corporate profits are the investments made to make them even richer. Capitalist manipulate stock prices to further their gains.

A little history here folks. Since the 1980's, the largest component for corporate income has come from stock-based pay. Before this time, most corporate leaders made most of their income from salaries, just like the regular folk. This means that corporate leaders have an incentive to see stock prices rise in value. The good old fashion way to do this is to produce better products leading to greater sales and, thus, increasing the value of the corporation. But here goes. In 1982 the Securities and Exchange Commission loosened the rules in regard to stock manipulation. This has led to an increase in stock buybacks by corporations increasing share prices. Harvard Business Review has reported that in recent years America's largest companies have devoted a whopping 54 percent of their profits to buying back shares, therefore, reducing the number of outstanding shares and raising the value of the shares they hold.

Companies buying their own shares? Why would they do that, you ask? Simple, to push the stock price higher, therefore, benefitting the senior managers who are all paid in stock. This takes money away from R&D and building new factories. More importantly, it takes away paying you overtime for all the hours you work. Just one reason why the stock market is soaring while the economy is stagnant. Some have put the figure of corporate stock buybacks at a staggering $7 trillion in the past decade alone. $7 TRILLION.

Here's two graphic examples of corporate greed. Low-wage king Wal-Mart in the past ten years has spent almost $65 billion in stock buybacks. This accounts for approximately 47% of their profits. That's $6.5 billion per year. That money could have given Wal-Mart's 1.4 million workers a $4,670 per year raise. But heavens, no, that's blasphemous! This $6.5 billion per year is also the equivalent to what Wal-Mart costs U.S. taxpayers each year in the form of food stamps, Medicaid, subsidized housing and other public assistance to their impoverished workers. That's right, two words that should never be said in the same sentence, impoverished and worker.

Further up the wage scale is that once scion of innovation, IBM. IBM's legacy was once one of investing in basic research. Why do that when you can pour an astounding $117.5 billion in stock buybacks since 2003. This is the new 21st century; IBM at its best, spending over 89 percent of its profits in stock buybacks with the sole purpose of propping up their stock prices and cash in on the gains.

What else could have been done with the total $6.9 TRILLION in stock manipulations perpetrated by greedy corporations you ask? Well, how about this, forgiving the $1 trillion of student debt holding back the purchasing power of young Americans. Fund the maintenance of our crumbling infrastructure which looms at $3.6 trillion. This would alleviate the backlog on our roads, bridges, dams, schools, and all the rest of our public infrastructure. Or how about this, use the annual $690 billion to put back to work the 9 million Americans who are unemployed at 2.5 times the pitiful median wage of $28,000 per year. So please, don't buy that crap that higher wages or a few more hours of overtime for you and your fellow workers are going to bankrupt your companies.

Bain & Co. calls the current situation a "capital superabundance." We've seen a tripling of global capital since 1990 and an overall stagnation of the underlying economy. As this glut of financial capital continues to grow, new technologies are reducing a demand for this capital. In the good old days, you needed billions to finance a new steel mill. But new companies are not as capital intensive. They just don't need the huge amount of initial capital that was once needed. Great example of this is Amazon. The start-up cost was approximately $1 million. Today they show over $136 billion in sales. This has caused what Bain & Co. calls a shift of power from "owners of capital" to "owners of ideas." You can argue that in the 21st century it's not capital accumulation that spurs on economic growth, but rather innovation and in increase in demand. The key to growth is what I have said before, include as many people in the process of innovation and consumption.

The workers are the economy. By increasing wages, you increase demand. Increase demand and you increase jobs, wages and innovation. But, in actuality, the more hours you work for less pay, you hurt not only yourself but also the overall economy. This serves only to depress wages, increase unemployment, and reduce demand and innovation. So we need to get in the ear of the decision makers. Most notably, the President. He hears from corporate executives and lobbyist about how raising the minimum wage and overtime threshold would be bad. They are right, it would be bad, bad for you. Workers need to mobilize, get on the same page. Workers need to fight together, instead of fighting against each other. It only serves the purposes of the very rich to have the bottom 90% fighting amongst itself. Fighting for mere scraps while they sit back in their corporate jets or yachts and laugh. Laugh all the way to the bank!

CHAPTER THREE

21St Century Presidents

The United States of America during much of the 20th century was seen as the preeminent symbol of both western modernity and the bastion of democracy. Its place in the world was unchallenged. Sure, there were some hitches in presidential elections during the 20th century. The 1948 election for instance, when the Chicago Daily Tribune ran its front page proclamation that Dewey defeats Truman. Oops. Truman won. 1960 election between Kennedy and Nixon being another. Allegations that the Kennedy camp fixed the vote in both Texas and Illinois. Then, of course, when Nixon does get a chance to be president in 1968 and again in 1972, he manages to disgrace the office like no other before him in the 20th century. One word, Watergate. So you see, heading into the 21st century and its first presidential election in 2000, we shouldn't have been so surprised by the wacky, and some would say, sinister result.

Bush vs. Gore, the 2000 election, one for the ages. What a way to usher in a century! The incumbent Vice-President Al Gore, won the candidacy of the Democratic Party. No surprise there. George W. Bush won the Republican candidacy with a victory over John McCain in the Republican primaries. Bush won with a campaign that focused on "compassionate conservativism." This included a greater role for the federal government in funding education, along with large reductions in the income and capital gains tax rates. It was a rather decisive victory for Bush in his battle to become the Republican candidate, while Gore won the Democratic nomination in a walkover. The only person to challenge him in the Democratic primaries was New Jersey Senator, "Dollar" Bill Bradley. Gore went on to win every state in the primary season. The candidates were chosen, and the race was on.

When looking back on the campaign, you see that the parties had grown more similar on some issues. It was a case of a more consensual political environment. Drug usage was condemned by both. The issue of abortion was largely ignored. And Vietnam, which hung over elections in the past, was now gone. But philosophic differences between the parties still remained. The republican's instincts led them to seek solutions through the actions of private entities or through the marketplace. They advocated for less government intervention in our economy. Whereas, the democrats consistently looked for governmental solutions to help our economy. The previous Clinton Administration was able to produce a budget surplus, and both parties were looking to capitalize on that. The Bush team was calling for across-the-board tax cuts, while Team Gore wanted new government programs and a more targeted tax-cut program.

There were other differences as well. In dealing with the issue of education, Bush called for state programing and testing. He also supported government vouchers to be used for private school tuitions. Gore called for new federal programs that would recruit new teachers and rebuild our schools. The issue of how to deal with Social Security brought two very different approaches as well. Bush wanted individuals to be able to invest part of their tax payment into a private investment account of their choosing. Gore called for transfers from other government programs into the Social Security trust fund.

When you look at this election, the main question should not be," How did Bush win?" It should definitely be "How the hell did Gore lose?" The economy, which is usually the largest influencer on voters, was in its largest period of prosperity in American history! This prosperity happened during a Democratic administration. A Democratic administration where Gore served as Vice-President. The second biggest influencer is the popularity of the incumbent president. President Clinton had a whopping 60% approval rate as he was leaving office. The Labor Day before the election, all these factors led pundits and academic experts to predict a unanimous Gore victory. The only disagreement came when predicting the size of that victory. The victory predicted ranged from 51%-60% for Gore.

But mistakes were obviously made. Duh. Gore had a burden when dealing with President Clinton in his campaign. There were obvious ethical questions surrounding Clinton due to his impeachment and affair with a White House intern, Monica Lewinsky. For the most part Clinton was sent to the sidelines by Gore, hoping to distance himself from the whole mess. But he sidelined a president with an exit approval rating of 60%. Gore miss stepped when dealing with the economic prosperity associated with the Clinton years. He barely mentioned past economic prosperity while out on the campaign trail. Gore chose to focus his attention and the attention of the voters on his future plans for the economy. He never hitched his wagon to the Clinton success. He subsequently failed to convince voters that continued prosperity depended on Democratic governance. In fact, Gore did very little to focus voters' attention on any Democratic achievements. He failed to put the election into a broader context by neglecting the Clinton Administration's record of achievement along with the achievements of the Democratic Party as a whole. He also neglected to use the Republican's record in Congress. The Republicans held majorities in both Houses in the prior six years. He never mentioned the role the Republican Congress played in blocking reforms to Social Security, the environment, abortion, and gun rights. Gore never promoted a partisan appeal among Democrats. In fact, he stayed away from mentioning the Democratic Party in three televised debates with Bush. This led to voter suppression among registered Democrats, especially among lower-income voters whose turnout was lower than in previous elections. Bush used the debates to commend the Democratic Party and played up his ability to deal with the opposition party. Bush was also deemed superior on most individual character traits, especially honesty and leadership. But nobody could have predicted what was to happen on Election Day 2000.

The battleground states for this election were Florida, Pennsylvania, Missouri, Wisconsin, Ohio, and Michigan. Bush felt he had Texas in his pocket and with a win in Florida (brother Jeb was the Florida Governor), he would sweep through the south and head to victory. A loss in Florida would necessitate running the table on the remaining battleground states. It became clear that Florida would be the key state in declaring a winner in this election when Gore was declared the winner in Michigan and then later Pennsylvania.

Let's focus on Florida and the sequence of events as it unfolded on election night 2000.

- **7:48 pm:** Associated Press, CNN, and all of the major television networks declare Vice-President Al Gore the winner in Florida.

- **8:47 pm:** After winning the states of Michigan, Illinois, and Pennsylvania, and with his anticipated win in California, broadcasters begin to talk as if Al Gore has won the election.

- **9:31 pm:** Bush's chief strategist, Karl Rove, takes to the airwaves to dispute the networks call of Gore as the winner in Florida.

- **9:55 pm:** Bush is shown on TV calmly asserting that his people in Florida assure him that when all the votes are counted there, he will win the state. Moments later, the networks now report that Florida is "too close to call."

- **11:47 pm:** The two candidates are now actually tied with 242 electoral votes apiece. This only emphasized the fact that Florida with its 25 electoral votes would be the deciding state for victory.

- **1:50 am:** With 95 percent of Florida's votes counted, it is reported that Bush leads by 38,000 votes.

- **1:55 am:** A mere five minutes later, with 96 percent of the votes in, Bush's lead falls to 30,000 votes.

- **2:18 am:** The Television networks once again declare a winner in Florida, but this time they call Bush the winner. They now begin to call George W. Bush the new President-Elect.

- **2:30 am:** With all the networks calling it a win for Bush, Vice President Gore calls Bush to concede the election and to congratulate him on his victory.

- **3:00 am:** Gore's motorcade heads to War Memorial in Tennessee to meet with his supporters and publicly concede.

- **3:10 am:** With 99 percent of Florida's vote now counted, Bush's lead dwindles to 11,000 votes.

- **3:15 am:** Gore's advisors frantically call Gore and tell him to hold up on a public concession. The margin is dwindling, and it's too close to call.

- **3:26 am:** Dan Rather reports that on the Florida Secretary of State's website it is reporting that Bush's lead in Florida is now down to a mere 629 votes.

- **3:30 am:** Gore makes another call to Bush, only this time to recant his concession. Bush reportedly didn't take this too well. Gore, in fact, is overheard saying, "Well you don't have to get snippy!" Gore turns his motorcade around returning to his hotel without addressing his supporters.

- **4:04 am:** The TV networks flip-flop yet again and say that George Bush might not have won this election.

- **4:34 am:** The Attorney General for the State of Florida, Bob Butterworth, confirms that Florida law would require an automatic machine recount. He goes on to report that within his state many counties are reporting voter irregularities. This is most apparent in Palm Beach County with its use of a "butterfly ballot" design.

What a night indeed. Many Americans woke up the next day only to find that the election was not quite over just yet. Little would they know that it would take till December 12th to declare a winner in this very unusual election. If you think election night was crazy, it was nothing compared to the events and legal wrangling's that took place over the next two months in declaring a winner. Here are the highlights. It's lengthy but worth the time so please stay with me:

- Florida law calls for an automatic machine recount of the votes. Recount shows an even closer Bush lead of 327 votes (out of over 6 million plus votes casted in Florida).

- Florida law now allows Gore the option of "manual vote recounts" and says he can do it in the counties of his choosing. Gore chooses the heavy Democratic counties of Broward, Miami-Dade, Volusia, and Palm Beach.

- Florida law also required that the state's election results were to be certified by Florida's Secretary of State Katherine Harris (Bush's co-chair in his election efforts in Florida b/t/w) within 7 days of the election. This would be by November 14, 2000.

- 3 of the 4 counties could not complete their recount by the allotted deadline (Nov 14th).

- So on Nov 14th the Florida Circuit Court ruled that while Harris must respect the deadline, she could legally amend the certified results at her own discretion to reflect any late returns from the outstanding counties. (Did I not mention she was Bush's co-chair in his election efforts in Florida?)

- Harris announces that she would entertain late returns **only** if their tardiness was justified by each county in writing by 2pm the next day!

- All 3 counties sent an explanation by the appointed deadline set by Harris.

- Secretary Harris **rejected** the explanations and announced that the final Florida vote count would be announced on Saturday, November 18, 2000.

- On Nov 16th Gore and Palm Beach County filed for an injunction against Harris to prevent her from certifying the election until the 3 counties could finish their recounts.

- The Florida Supreme Court issued the injunction on Nov 17th and on Nov 21 ruled that Secretary Harris must allow the counties until Nov 26th to finish their recounts. Whew! Getting there, but not quite yet.

- Miami-Dade County stopped their recount because they felt it would be impossible to complete it by the new Nov 26th deadline.

- Gore sort and failed to get a court order for Miami-Dade to continue their recount.

- On Nov 26th with 537 votes separating Bush and Gore, Secretary Harris certified the election for Bush. (I did mention she was co-chair for the Bush election efforts in Florida, right?)

- So, on Nov 27th Gore sues Harris alleging that the certified results were illegitimate because the recount process was not yet completed. Of course, he did.

- When a local Court dismissed the suit, Gore appealed to the Florida Supreme Court.

- December 8th (it's December now and no new President yet) Florida Supreme Court ruled all votes casted but not counted by voting machines (under-votes) must be manually recounted if they haven't been already.

- It was found that many votes were not counted because of defects in punch-card ballots, which would become known as "hanging-chads."

- Bush appeals this decision, of course, to the United States Supreme Court which starts to review the case on Dec 9th.

- On December 12, 2000, The United States Supreme Court rules by a narrow 5-4 majority that George W. Bush was the new President of the United States. Gore was out of options.

This was the only election to be decided by the United States Supreme Court. Oh, in case you are wondering, the party makeup within the Supreme Court at that time was five Republicans and four Democrats. Hmmm. Seems the Court voted along party lines. Politics in the Court? The two wings that made up this court were the conservative Republican wing consisting of Chief Justice William Rehnquist, along with Justices Antonin Scalia, Clarence Thomas, Sandra Day O'Connor, and Anthony Kennedy. The liberal Democratic wing consisted of Justices John Paul Stevens, Ruth Bader Ginsburg, Stephen Breyer, and David Souter. It is interesting to look behind the curtain to see the inner workings of the Supreme Court as it weighed the outcome of this election.

A little background information on how this all started. Bush's team turned to the Supreme Court days before Thanksgiving and asked the highest court to end this "circus" and stop the recount. The Bush team argued that the recount violated an 1887 Federal law which prohibited a State from changing the election rules after the actual date of that election. They argued that by getting the Florida State Supreme Court involved, they usurped the Florida Legislative's exclusive powers to set the procedures for selecting electors as provided by Article II of the U.S. Constitution. Their third and most pertinent point as it turned out, was the selective recounts violated constitutional guarantees of Due Process and Equal Protection, meaning that by using different criteria for recounting ballots, it did not give equal rights to all voters.

The Writ of Certiorari went initially to Justice Kennedy who was assigned to consider all emerging motions from the states of Florida, Georgia and Alabama. Kennedy, who was said to relish the Pomp and Circumstance of the Court, quickly urged the Court to take this on. He suggested that the Court was absolutely the essential arbiter of such weighty matters.

Initially, Kennedy would concede that Bush would face an uphill battle. Under Court rules, Kennedy needed three other Justices to agree in order for the Court to hear the case. He turned to his fellow conservatives, and they all quickly signed on.

The Court set a quick calendar. Normally, arguments are set months in advance. But in this case, briefs were due in four days and oral arguments were set for December 1st, only a week away. Both clerks and Justices for the conservative wing gave up vacation plans and stuck close to the Court. The liberal wing meanwhile could only watch the events unfold with dismay. They did however, hold out some hope after hearing Kennedy's initial skepticism about Bush's chances. One liberal clerk remembers, "We changed our minds every five minutes about whether the fix was in!" Gore at this point felt it was inconceivable that the Court would get involved, much less ultimately losing the election on a 5-4 vote! The liberals questioned why the Court would even agree to consider the Florida ruling at all, unless it was to overturn it and shut down the recount with Bush in the lead. The liberal wing actually set out to draft a dissent before the case was argued in court. The liberal clerks, as well as the Gore team, felt that the case would rest with Justices Kennedy and O'Connor. Based on previous rulings, these Justices were seen to be more moderate than the others who comprised the conservative wing. For instance, O'Connor once went against the Republican call to reverse Roe v. Wade when she provided the swing vote in Planned Parenthood v. Casey (1992). Kennedy once voted to uphold both abortion rights and later gay rights, definitely breaking from the conservative wing's position.

Kennedy had detractors on both sides. The conservatives had problems with Kennedy breaking away from their agenda, and the liberals saw him as both pompous and grandiose. Or at least that's how the liberal **clerks** viewed him. To the clerks, he was a figure of ridicule and scorn. So it was under these circumstances that the Court first heard oral arguments by both parties. After arguments were heard, the justices met for their usual conference. Justice Stevens represented one position, Justice Scalia the other. Stevens wanted to stay out of the fray altogether and let the political process play out on its own. Scalia wanted to overrule the Florida Supreme Court's decision and effectively call the election for Bush. At this point neither side had the votes. So, on December 4th, Chief Justice Rehnquist drafted a ruling to ask the Florida Supreme Court to clarify its ruling. On the surface this action by Rehnquist seemed to serve both sides. It would spare the liberals a divisive loss and it would serve to eat up Gore's time, therefore the conservatives would win without looking partisan in the process.

But it couldn't be that easy, could it? To the surprise of everyone, the Florida Supreme Court ruled 4-3 in ordering a statewide recount of all under-votes. There were approximately 61,000 such under-votes that the Florida voting machines seemed to miss. The Florida Court did not set a standard for the recount letting each county set its own. When the U.S. Supreme Court clerks saw the televised images of Florida officials inspecting punch-card ballots, looking for hanging, dimpled, or pregnant chads, they all knew the case would be heading back their way.

Bush, once again, asked the Court to stay the decision and stop the recount. Justice Scalia wanted to grant the stay immediately even without Gore's response. Why was Scalia in such a rush? Perhaps it had to do with the fact that Gore was gaining on Bush in the recount. Gore's team was convinced that by Monday (Dec 11th) he would pull away. But Scalia maintained that all the recounts were illegitimate. He felt that continuing the recount would only serve to cast a cloud over Bush's legitimacy when he is ultimately sworn in as President. Many of the clerks were surprised at how hard Scalia was pushing his own obviously partisan agenda. However Scalia's wish was not granted. Instead Chief Justice Rehnquist scheduled a conference on the matter for the next day at 10am. At the conference clear lines were drawn, the five conservatives wanting the recount to stop while the four liberals wanted the political system to play out. But the Court granted the stay and ordered that no more votes were to be counted. They set oral arguments once again for Monday, December 11th.

The Gore team was crushed. But they still held a slim hope that they could sway either Kennedy or O'Connor or both to their side. The liberal clerks, however, sensed it was over. As far as O'Connor, the clerks reported that she was heard at an Election Day party voicing her dismay over an apparent Gore victory. Some clerks thought that perhaps O'Connor would step aside given her vocal support for Bush. No such luck for them. O'Connor stood firm and sent a sealed memo to the other Justices stating she felt the Florida Supreme Court improperly usurped that state's legislative power. The Gore team actually debated asking O'Connor to recuse herself, but they decided not to, hoping she would lean towards them to prove her fairness. Fat chance Al.

Kennedy agreed with O'Connor's assessment but felt that that argument alone would not be enough. In a memo to his colleagues, Kennedy argued that by evaluating ballots under different standards, a violation was committed under the Fourteenth Amendment's Equal Protection Clause. This was an argument that has always been narrowly viewed by the Court. It had been applied only under circumstances of blatant discrimination that was both intentional and irreversible. In fact, when the Bush team originally petitioned the Court, they used the Equal Protection Clause argument and that argument was turned down. But Kennedy was undeterred. The liberals felt that if the question is the fairness of the recount, the solution was simple. Send it back to the Florida Supreme Court and ask them to set a more uniform standard for recounts across all counties. Kennedy was seen being swayed by Justice Breyer's argument to send it back to Florida, but Kennedy flipped back to the conservative side within a half-hour. What happened during that half-hour, you ask? Well, it was reported that Kennedy met with Scalia and his own hand-picked right-wing clerks. Breyer felt that they had worked Kennedy over and brought him back to their side.

Rehnquist wrote the majority opinion reversing the Florida Court on jurisdictional and equal-protection grounds. Stevens wrote the principal dissent. Both Stevens and Ginsburg denied that equal-protection applied in this case. He chastised the Court for holding the Justices of the Florida Supreme Court up to ridicule. Scalia came back and complained about the tone of some of the dissents. He felt that they were attacking the Court. He was especially harsh in his complaints toward Ginsburg over her "Al Sharpton" footnote. Ginsburg took it out. The clerks saw this as a bullying technique by Scalia and felt that Ginsburg lacked courage.

The majority decision was announced at 10am December 12th, 2000. Gore's lawyers read him the ruling, and they concluded that the Court never gave him a chance. Justice Breyer was especially upset by the decision. He called it "the most outrageous, indefensible thing the Court had ever done." Souter lamented that if only he had one more day, he felt he could have convinced Kennedy to come to his side. Meanwhile, O'Connor expressed surprise over the level of anger that greeted the decision. Many felt that this particular decision put an end to any hope Scalia had in becoming Chief Justice. The recount was now over, the election was over. George W. Bush was the new forty-third President of the United States. Whew. That was easy!

George W. Bush, the nation's forty-third president, served two terms. He is the son of George W.H. Bush, the nation's forty-first president. George W. was also a two-term Republican governor from the State of Texas. He was a graduate of both Yale University and Harvard Business School. Before becoming Governor, Bush had worked in the Texas oil industry and for a time he was an owner of the Texas Rangers Major League Baseball team. This was the man that emerged victorious from the 2000 election debacle. He was declared the winner in the Electoral College but had lost the popular vote to Al Gore. His victory, which was granted to him by the U.S. Supreme Court, made many skeptical of their new president. However, he did enter office in 2001 with an overall Gallup poll approval rating of 57% (Feb 2001). His approval rating would dip to a low of 25% three times during his two terms, and he would exit office with a rating of only 34%. However, he would see his ratings skyrocket to a high of 90% in September 2001 with the handling of the aftermath of the 9/11 attacks. It was a roller coaster ride indeed.

No discussion on George W. Bush can be had without talking about that unparalleled moment in U.S. history, the September 11, 2001 attacks on the World Trade Center, the Pentagon and the downed plane in Shanksville, Pennsylvania. For those of us who are native New Yorkers and having lost family and friends in the attacks on the World Trade Center, it is a moment that is indelibly marked on our consciousness. But as we move away in time from that catastrophe, it becomes somewhat easier (somewhat) to discuss both the event and Bush's handling of the aftermath. But what is still somewhat sensitive to discuss is the handling of information Bush received before the attacks occurred. How much did Bush know before the attack? The question isn't could he have stopped the attacks, that's unknowable. But he was given several warnings that al-Qaeda was planning attacks on U.S. soil and with that info, Bush did nothing. That is a fact. Now I don't want this to be a book about 9/11 (perhaps at a later time, I will). But I'll quickly highlight some of the information gathered over the years as it pertains to the time before the attacks.

There is always the infamous CIA Presidential Daily Brief (or PDB for those in the know) of August 6, 2001 which stated, "Bin Laden determined to strike in the U.S." Ignored. But what we now know is that the CIA repeatedly and urgently warned the White House that an attack was coming starting in the spring of 2001. In a series of interviews conducted by producers of Showtime's documentary *The Spymasters*, George Tenet, the Director of the CIA at that time, reveals in detail meetings with the Bush team and warning them about impending attacks. Ignored. In the spring of 2001 according to Tenet, he and Cofer Black, the Chief of the CIA's Counterterrorism Center, pitched a plan called "Blue Sky Paper" to the new Bush security team. The plan called for a covert CIA and military campaign to end the threat posed by al-Qaeda. Tenet says the Bush team responded with, "We are not ready to consider this. We don't want the clock to start ticking yet." Tenet took this to mean that the Bush administration wanted to avoid a paper trail about any warnings pertaining to al-Qaeda and terrorist attacks in the U.S. at that time.

Fast forward to July 10th, 2001. Richard Blee, the head of the CIA's al-Qaeda unit, urgently informs Black, and later Tenet, that according to multiple credible sources an attack is at hand. Tenet recalls calling Condoleezza Rice, Bush's National Security Adviser, requesting an urgent meeting. Information about significant attacks by al-Qaeda in the upcoming weeks or months were relayed to Rice and her team. The attacks would be both spectacular and multiple, as reported by Tenet. When asked by Rice what needed to be done, Black slammed his palm on the desk and responded, "We need to go on a wartime footing now." Response, ignored. The plan of action advised by the CIA that day in July was finally put into effect, September 17th, 2001. More than two weeks **AFTER** the attacks!

Getting back to the infamous PDB (see how I did that?) of August 6, 2001, the one warning that Bin Laden was determined to attack the U.S., Bush was on his ranch in Crawford, Texas. None of his senior advisers were present for the briefing. Rice would later describe that particular PDB to be "very vague" and "very non-specific." She remembered it to be "mostly historical." But after a great struggle, the 9/11 Commission was able to get these documents declassified. The commission revealed that the President received thirty-six PDF's that year relating to al-Qaeda and Bin Laden. This PDF (August 6, 2001) however, was the first to specifically warn of a Bin Laden plan to target the U.S.

Tenet recalls that he was becoming agitated by the chatter he was picking up that summer, along with Bush's lack of attention to the matter. He arranged for another CIA briefing with the president later that August. Bush was still at his ranch in Texas, and Tenet tried to get the President's attention to what he perceived as an impending danger. When the agents finished their briefing of the president, Tenet reports the president responded, "All right. You've covered your ass now." And nothing was done. Ignored. I hate doing this, but it's all for the record. Meanwhile, Bush has never addressed this situation himself. He only reluctantly agreed to cooperate with the 9/11 Commission. The arrangement was that only two commission members could be present at a White House meeting where Bush would be questioned for no more than an hour. He would be questioned without being put under oath, with no notes to be taken, and with Vice-President Dick Cheney present. What is arguable is the question of whether the attacks could have been stopped. What can't be argued are the actions that Bush and his team failed to take to prevent these attacks. But like the old saying, "Hindsight is 20-20." Or is it in this situation?

On the morning of Tuesday, September 11, 2001, President Bush was scheduled to participate in a reading demonstration at Emma E. Booker Elementary School in Sarasota, Florida. He was there to read the book *The Pet Goat* to a second-grade class at the school as well as promote his new proposed education bill. The following timeline begs the question, why? Why did President Bush go ahead with the reading? For the purposes of this book, I will focus on the movements and actions (or non-actions) of our President as it pertains to the events as they unfolded on September 11, 2001.

Various accounts have the President leaving the resort he was staying at anywhere between 8:30 to 8:39am. There was a distance of nine miles between the resort and the school. The police had shut down any traffic along the route, so it was estimated that the drive would take approximately fourteen minutes. Most accounts have the President arriving at the school shortly before 9:00am. Why is the time when he left the resort and arrived at the school important? Because this is the crucial time that Bush was told or should have been told about the first attack on the towers. Official reports, and Bush himself, state that he was not informed until he arrived at the school and was inside of the building. However, there are at least four other reports which state Bush was informed while in route to the school. Remember, the first pictures of the burning World Trade Center was broadcast live over network TV at 8:48 am. Is it conceivable that the world found out about this incident before our President did? And is it conceivable that our President would remain in the dark for an additional ten minutes before being told?

How is it that others who were part of his motorcade had information about the attacks? Kia Baskerville, a CBS news producer traveling with the Bush motorcade that morning, received word about a plane crash as they headed to the planned event. Senior Presidential Communication Officer Thomas Herman said, "Just as we were arriving at the school, I received a notification from our communications center than (sic) an airliner had struck one of the towers." Others at the school awaiting the arrival of President Bush report they were aware of the crash before the motorcade arrived. Tampa Bay's Channel 8 reporter, Jackie Barron, says at about 8:50am she was on the phone with her mother and informed about the crash. Brian Goff, a Fox reporter from Tampa, heard the news via his cell phone. Associated Press reporter, Sonia Ross, was also told of the crash by phone from a colleague. Florida Congressman Dan Miller was informed by an aide at approximately 8:55am, minutes before Bush arrived at the school function. How could Bush have remained ignorant of any attack? His limousine was loaded with the latest in communication equipment. There seems to have been plenty of time and also plenty of opportunities to inform the president before his arrival.

On the television news program, Meet the Press, on 9/16/01 Vice-President Dick Cheney said the following, "The Secret Service has an arrangement with the FAA. They had open lines after the World Trade Center was…" He never finished his sentence, but you can predict with certainty that the next word would have been "hit." His statement makes it clear that the Secret Service knew the extent of the situation in New York well before 9:00 am. It is also known that by the time Bush arrived at the school, authorities were aware that three planes had been hijacked. Another report was given by US Navy Captain Deborah Loewer, the director of the White House Situation Room, who was traveling with the motorcade. She reports that she received word from an assistant back in Washington about the first crash. She says that as soon as the cars arrived at Booker, she ran quickly over to Bush. She is quoted as saying, "It's a good thing the Secret Service knows who I am" as she approached Bush, telling the president that an aircraft had "impacted the World Trade Center. This is all we know."

With knowledge of three planes already hijacked and one of them crashing into the World Trade Center, who would assume that Flight 11's crash was just an accident? But according to official reports, that is precisely what they claim. Although there are several different "official" reports, all of them stress that Bush wasn't told until he arrived inside of the building (in direct contrast to the report given by Captain Loewer). Some reports have Chief of Staff, Andrew Card, telling the President first. While other reports state it was advisor, Karl Rove, who first informs the president. I could go on and on about information pertaining to when Bush was notified. Logic says that his advisors were aware, therefore, Bush was aware while in route to the school. At least I would hope so. With the news that three planes were hijacked and one of the hijacked planes crashed into the World Trade Center, I would hope that the President's advisors were well aware before millions of us saw the burning towers on TV. No?

Bush made some curious statements in the weeks and months following the attacks. He stated on December 4, 2001, "I was sitting outside the classroom, waiting to go in, and I saw an airplane hit the tower. The TV was obviously on," (jeez I hope so). "…But I was whisked off there, I didn't have much time to think about it." Hmm, interesting, because there was no film footage of the first plane hitting the Tower until at least the following day. Was the TV indeed off, and was the president experiencing a clairvoyant moment? Perhaps he was thinking of the second plane which many

Americans witnessed live? Hmmm…no, because he states he was inside the classroom when Card approached him and whispered in his ear that the second plane hit. What's strange is that his advisors never corrected him or even stopped him from telling the same version four weeks later (January 5, 2002) and again on the first anniversary of the attack September 11, 2002. Not so surprising, I guess, is that Bush has never been asked to explain these statements.

What is known, however, is that at 9:07am, Andrew Card is seen on camera approaching the president and whispering something in his ear. Card tells the president: "A second plane hit the towers. America is under attack." Descriptions vary as to how Bush reacted to the news. It's said that the president "blanched" [Richmond-Times Dispatch, 10/01/02] "the color drained from the president's face." [AP 9/12/01]. "…visibly tense and serious." [Time 9/12/01]. Bush later recalled his own reaction, "I am very aware of the cameras. I'm trying to absorb that knowledge. I have nobody to talk to. I'm sitting in the midst of a classroom of little kids, listening to a children's story, and I realize I'm the Commander in Chief, and the country has come under attack." [Telegraph 12/16/01, CBS 11/1/02]. Asked again what he thought after hearing the news he said, "We're at war and somebody has dared attack us and we're going to do something about it. I realized I was in a unique setting to receive a message that somebody attacked us… [I]t became evident that we were, you know, that the world had changed." [CBS 9/11/02]. But what does Commander in Chief, President Bush, do when informed that America was indeed under attack? One word, nothing. That's right, nothing. He didn't say a word, didn't ask questions or give any orders. He didn't ask who attacked us or whether there were more attacks anticipated He didn't ask if any military plans were underway or even if there should be any military plans underway. Fact is, President Bush knew nothing of what was happening outside of that classroom. But hey, even his Secret Service detail thought little of the attacks because they didn't think it was prudent to whisk the president away knowing the country was under attack.

Here's another point. Military pilots must first have White House approval from the President before any civilian plane can be struck down. But if retaliatory strikes were needed, Bush was not available to give the order. Several fighters had, indeed, been dispatched to defend New York City. The pilot of one of the planes in pursuit of Flight 175 (the second plane to hit the towers) noted that it wouldn't have mattered if they caught up to the plane because only Bush could order the strike and he was unavailable in the classroom. Interestingly, the Secret Service did burst into the White House office of Vice-President Cheney and whisked him away to safety in a bunker under the White House. This timeline is also disputed. It varies from 9:06am till past 9:30am. The one eyewitness, David Bohrer, a White House photographer, says it happened just after 9:00am. Hmm, serious enough to secure the Vice-President, but let the President stay in the classroom and continue to read with the children?

Bush does eventually leave, again with conflicting times given. Some reports say as early as 9:12am, others at 9:16am. When he leaves the classroom, he stops for a photo-op and when asked by a reporter, "Mr. President, are you aware of the reports of the plane crash in New York? Is there anything..." Bush interrupts to say, "I'll talk about it later." All in all, Bush's actions during and after the classroom photo-op show that he proceeded in a calm and deliberate manner, in no hurry to get out and attend to this seemingly urgent national security matter. When Bush's Advisor, Karl Rove, was asked why Bush did not leave after Card informed him of the second plane he said, "Without all the facts at hand, George Bush had no intention of upsetting the schoolchildren who had come to read for him." [MSNBC 10/29/02]. He went on to say, "The President thought for a second or two about getting up and walking out of the room. But the drill was coming to a close, and he didn't want to alarm the children." Really?? Upset a room full of children vs. acting like the Commander-In-Chief given the security risks and the importance of the President being informed and making decisions for our country? The fact is that one drill in the classroom had just ended, and it afforded the President an ideal opportunity to excuse himself from the room and head out to the airport. One of the reasons Booker Elementary School was chosen for this photo-op in the first place was its proximity to an airport. Sarasota-Bradenton International Airport was only 3.5 miles away from the school. The fact is, hijackers could have crashed a plane into Bush's publicized location, putting the President and all others, including schoolchildren, in grave danger.

You think that's a stretch? Well, what if I told you that two of the 9/11 hijackers came to Sarasota on September 7, the day that Bush's schedule was publicly announced [White House 9/7/01]. The Secret Service was also well aware of a strange request made by several middle- eastern men earlier that morning (9/11). In the early morning hours of 9/11 a van with several middle-eastern men identifying themselves as journalists, pulled up to the guard station of the resort where the President was staying. They claimed they had a scheduled poolside interview with the President, and they asked for a certain Secret Service agent by name. That message was relayed to Secret Service agents located inside of the resort. The agents said they were unware of any request for a poolside interview and that they have never heard of the agent that they asked for. They told the men to contact the President's public relations office in Washington, D.C. and had the van turned away. [Longboat Observer, 9/26/01]. Was this a foiled assassination attempt? Another stretch? Well, consider this. The Secret Service was well aware that two days earlier Ahmed Shah Massoud, leader of Afghanistan's Northern Alliance, had been murdered by a similar ruse. After repeated requests for an interview with Massoud, it was finally arranged for September 9, 2001. Two North African men showed up with credentials posing as journalists from "Arabic News International." As the interview got underway, a bomb hidden in their camera exploded killing both journalists and Massoud [Newsday, 10/26/01]. This assassination was later believed to have been timed to remove the Taliban's most respected and popular opponent in anticipation of the backlash that would occur after the 9/11 attacks. The

Northern Alliance would go on to blame al-Qaeda and ISI, Pakistan's secret service for the attacks [Newsday, 9/15/01]. There was another report made later that morning (9/11) by a man waiting for the Presidential motorcade to pass on its way to the school. He states while standing at the Sarasota bay front, he saw two middle-eastern men in a dilapidated van "screaming out their windows 'down with Bush' and raising their fists in the air." When the man was questioned by the FBI, it could not be determined if they were the same two men who came to see the President earlier that morning. I guess Sarasota has an abundance of vans driven in the early morning by middle-eastern men in their community.

Bush and his motorcade eventually heads to the airport. They leave the school at 9:35am (not disputed), and at 9:37am Flight 77 crashes into the Pentagon. Bush is notified as his motorcade nears the airport. He makes a call to his Vice-President, and it's reported that during this call Bush orders all flights within the U.S. to be grounded [Sarasota Magazine, 11/01]. But of course, there are other reports to the contrary. [USA Today 10/02/02] states that is was FAA administrator, Ben Sliney, who made the decision without consulting anyone. Anyhow, after closely scrutinizing all the baggage before loading onto Air Force One, takeoff is reported at 9:55am.

Communications Director Dan remembered, "It was like a rocket. For a good ten minutes, the plane was going almost straight up." [CBS, 9/11/02]. Incredibly, Air Force One, carrying the President of the United States, took off without any military fighter protection. None, zip, nada. There was plenty of time during Bush's prolonged visit to the school to arrange for fighters to get to Sarasota. It makes sense on two fronts, to protect the President and Air Force One, but also to protect Bush on the ground before he leaves the school. Was it possible you're wondering? Well, how about the fact that Florida has two bases on 24-hour alert. Each base is capable in getting airborne in less than five minutes: Homestead Air Station, 185 miles from Sarasota, and Tyndall Air Station, 235 miles from Sarasota. Both stations reportedly had its highest readiness status on 9/11. Fighters with the same alert status had left bases and traveled the same distance to reach Washington D.C. well before 10:00am. Why were the fighters delayed in Florida? Military planes should have been over Sarasota at the latest 9:35am, the time Bush left the school. As unfathomable as it was to think, Air Force One was in the air for several hours before fighter jets arrived to protect it.

An administration official said, "The object seemed to be simply to get the President airborne and out of the way." [Telegraph 12/16/01] This really makes no sense when you consider that we are being attacked by air. At this time, there were reports that as many as 11 planes might have been hijacked. There are almost 3,000 planes over U.S. airspace when Air Force One takes off. Almost half of the planes are in the Florida region where Bush was. [St. Petersburg Times, 9/7/02] Another thing that's debated, did the Secret Service have knowledge of a threat made towards Bush and Air Force One just minutes after Bush left Booker Elementary School? Karl Rove, flying with Bush on Air Force One, confirmed that a dangerous threat was made before the plane took off. "...they also made it clear they wanted to get us up quickly, and they wanted to get us to a high altitude, because there had been a specific threat made to Air Force One...A declaration that Air Force One was a target and said in a way that they called it credible." [New Yorker 10/01/01]

So, let's get the President up in the air? Up in the air without military air support? Does this seem like sound reasoning to you? What exactly is going on here? What are the people responsible for keeping our President safe, along with the people of the U.S. safe, actually thinking here? Wow, what a cluster-fuck of bad decision-making if you ask me. Or perhaps all of these threats were untrue as has been speculated by various news agencies? These bogus reports of threats could have been fashioned to support the decision to fly the president to two different Air Force Bases before returning to Washington, D.C. To fast forward, Air Force One finally lands at Andrews Air Force Base at 6:34pm escorted by two F-15's and one F-16. He is taken from the base by the Marine One helicopter and arrives at the White House shortly before 7:00pm. [CNN 9/12/01] About ten hours after the initial plane hits the World Trade Center out of reach and out of sight of the American public who just witnessed this horrific attack. The American public was left to wonder the whereabouts of our President, and what exactly was going on?

Bush did go on national television to address the nation at 8:30pm and spoke for about five minutes. [CNN, 9/12/01] In what would become known as the Bush Doctrine, he stated, "We will make no distinction between the terrorists who committed these acts and those who harbor them." [Washington Post, 1/27/02] Bush was to write in his diary that night, "The Pearl Harbor of the 21st century took place today…We think it was Osama bin Laden." [Washington Post 1/27/02]

There are many worthy criticisms of how the day of 9/11 was handled by Bush and his team, but there are very few criticisms on how Bush acted to assuage the feelings of fear that struck the nation in the days after the attacks. Two of these moments stand in time. The first was when President Bush stood atop the pile of wreckage at the World Trade Center with his arm around a firefighter vowing to get whoever perpetrated this attack. And the second being when he stepped to the mound at Yankee Stadium to throw out the first pitch, signaling a return to order and a show of strength by the President and by the nation. If you are old enough to remember those times, a lump has to come to your throat. We were fired up, and our President was also fired up. His humanness (if that's even a word) shone through. The man was hurting as we hurt, and he was ready to take action, like many of us would have if we were in his position. It was at this point that Bush had his highest approval ratings. (over 90%). This event defined his presidency like no other. What he knew and when he knew it is certainly critical when looking at this horrific event. But could it have been stopped? Would another attack have taken place instead? What's to gain from this type of thinking?

The Bush presidency had other successful moments as well. Bush enacted the biggest tax breaks in American history. He was making good on a campaign promise and also on remarks made in his acceptance speech. Bush was fortunate that in the late 1990's the federal government actually ran a budget surplus. (Imagine that??) The Brookings Institution called the surplus, "one of the supreme budgetary accomplishments in American history." The presidential campaign of 2000 came with different views on how to deal with this unique surplus situation. Some policymakers wanted to maintain the course and continue to build budget surpluses. But these policymakers were drowned out by the cries on how to spend the surplus. Bush and his team called for the surplus to be returned to the American public in the form of tax relief. He was quoted in his acceptance speech as saying,

"The last time taxes were this high as a percentage of our economy, there was good reason…We were fighting World War II. Today, our taxes fund a surplus. Some say that a growing federal surplus means Washington has more money to spend. But they have it backwards. The surplus is not the government's money. The surplus is the people's money."

So, the Economic Growth and Tax Relief Reconciliation Act of 2001 was enacted. The main focus of the act was to lower taxes for all Americans. Some of the cuts involved lowering the rates of the top four tax brackets by 3-4 points, along with adding a new 10 percent bracket for low income households. It also increased the standard deduction for married couples and doubled the Child Tax Credit. In order for the cuts to be made more politically palatable as well as conforming to procedural laws in the Senate, Congress designed the bill so that many of its provisions would expire on December 31, 2010. President Obama was in office when the tax cuts were set to expire in 2010. Obama extended the cuts for another two years. He wanted to avert a dramatic tax increase during troubling financial times. The fate of the Bush tax cuts was finally settled in 2012 when Congress decided which cuts would become permanent and which cuts would go. All told, 82 percent of the cuts made by the Bush administration were made permanent, while 18 percent were allowed to expire. Some feel that these tax cuts for low and middle-class Americans were a major policy victory for the Bush administration.

Another legislative highpoint for the Bush administration came when Bush signed into law major Medicare reform that included prescription drug benefits. Bush called the measure, "The greatest advance in healthcare coverage for America's seniors since the founding of Medicare." The $400 billion Medicare Prescription Drug Modernization Act was set up to provide much-needed help for seniors buying prescription drugs.

An economic highlight for the Bush Administration came when actions were taken by the administration to prevent a meltdown of the U.S. financial system in the fall of 2008. The main component of the action taken by the Bush Administration was the creation of the Troubled Asset Relief Program (TARP). This served to stabilize the financial sector and prevented its complete disappearance. There were other economic measures taken along with this program, the gist being that these immediate actions by Bush headed off a complete dismantling of our financial sector.

It would be negligent to not discuss Bush's decision to invade Iraq on March 20, 2003. The main reason given for the invasion was that Saddam Hussein had access to weapons of mass destruction (WMDs). There was fear that these weapons were in the hands of a madman and equally scary was that they could fall into the hands of enemy terrorist organizations. A very frightening thought indeed. In the end, there were no such weapons in Iraq, and any link made by the Bush administration between Saddam and al- Qaeda were unfounded. Many mistakes were made in this regard, including misinformation regarding Iraq's WMD capabilities, unwillingness to allow UN Inspectors more time to conclude weapons checks, no peremptory diplomacy that caused damage to the Atlantic Alliance, and the gross failure to anticipate what would happen in post-conflict Iraq. After the 9/11 attacks many in the Bush Administration thought Iraq was behind the attacks, therefore, so did the American public. It would soon become clear that this was not the case. The first order of business was the destruction of al-Qaeda in Afghanistan. Saddam and Iraq would quickly be put on the front burner, though. Bush clearly indicated that as soon as al-Qaeda was driven from Afghanistan, he would again turn his attention to Saddam and Iraq.

Hard to feel bad for Saddam. This is a man who used chemical weapons against his own people and against Iran during the 1980's. He also invaded a sovereign Kuwait and initiated a bloody war with Iran. He failed to comply with the UN Security Council on at least 10 resolutions aimed at ending his WMD programs. The Bush Administration felt that if the U.S. could bring about a regime change in Iraq (get rid of Saddam), it could create a new model of democracy in the Middle East. Democracy in the Middle East would be a game-changer according to the Bush Adminis-tration. It would bring stability to that area in the world, and also provide a safer environment for America's ally, Israel. A new regime in Iraq would allow the U.S. to remove troops from Saudi Arabia, and wait for it…have another friendly source for oil. There, I said it. Of course, oil played a part in this decision. Anyone who denies this has their heads in the Arabian sands.

You can never discount the fact that there was bad blood between Bush and Saddam. Saddam was said to have put out an assassination order against Bush's dad, George H.W. Bush while he was on a trip to the Middle East. I guess this was in retaliation for the butt whipping Papa Bush put on Saddam in the earlier Gulf War. The fact that Saddam, "tried to kill his dad," weighed heavily on the decision to go after Saddam and Iraq. It was considered "unfinished" business for the U.S. But the seeds for removing Saddam were planted before Bush ever took office. As far back as 1998 a neo-conservative organization known as "The Project for the New Amer-ican Century," wrote an open letter to then President Clinton arguing that Saddam and Iraq posed a major threat to the United States and was seen as a destabilizing force in the Middle East. This organization was formed in response to the decision made by President George H.W. Bush at the end of the Gulf War in 1991. Bush, Sr. showed restraint in limiting the coalition's victory to just driving the Iraqi forces out of Kuwait without completely destroying them and invading Iraq. Bush, Sr. felt to do this would exceed the UN mandate given and would have moved well beyond the support of the coalition. It would also go against the U.S.'s stated military mission to just remove Iraq from Kuwait.

In their open letter to President Clinton, the group urged the president to remove Saddam Hussein's regime from power, and they favored military actions because they viewed diplomacy as failing. This was the environment that confronted Bush when he entered the presidency in 2001. As for those neo-conservatives who urged Clinton to remove Saddam from power, many found their way into the Bush Administration. For instance, the neo-conservative roster included Donald Rumsfeld as Secretary of Defense, Paul Wolfowitz to be his deputy, along with Richard Perle, Douglas Feith, and Lewis "Scooter" Libby (really, there's only one "Scooter" and he played shortstop for the NY Yankees in the '40's and 50's, Phil Rizzuto.). All these men had high profile positions within the Administration. Let's not forget Vice-President Dick Cheney who was a strong ally to the neo-conservatives and their desire to use U.S. military power to remove Saddam from power in Iraq.

Bush was initially against an aggressive stance toward Saddam. But with the 9/11 attacks, all bets were off. There were serious discussions to attack Saddam right away, but it was decided that matters in Afghanistan with al-Qaeda were to be handled first. Bush did, however, direct the Defense Department to plan for an eventual war with Iraq. Many within the military voiced concerns about a U.S. attack on Iraq. While it's not unusual for the military and the White House to differ on matters, it is unusual, however, when the military publicly voices these concerns. The *Washington Post* cited "senior military officers" and "some top generals and admirals in the military establishment, including members of the Joints

Chiefs of Staff," who argued for a more cautious approach to Iraq. They believed that Iraq played no role in 9/11, and they felt containment had worked up till then. Another belief was that a military victory would be followed by a lengthy occupation of Iraq.

Members of Bush Sr.'s former Administration also voiced their concerns. This included Brent Scowcroft, Nation Security Advisor for Bush Sr., James Baker, former Secretary of State, and General Norman Schwarz-kopf, Commander of U.S. forces in the Gulf War in 1991. George H. Bush had resistance from within his own Administration as well. His Secretary of State, Colin Powell, argued to the President that a war with Iraq would destabilize the whole Middle East, and an American occupation would be seen as hostile by the Muslim world. He argued that if the President wanted to have a go with Iraq, we shouldn't do it alone, but instead we should recruit allies, preferably through the UN. Bush was not persuaded by Powell's arguments, but he did decide that a scheduled address to the UN on September 12th would be on Iraq. Both Rumsfeld and Cheney continued to press Bush to move against Saddam, and they said the U.S. didn't need a new resolution from the UN to do it.

In Bush's speech to the UN on September 12th, he stressed the credibility of the UN and the urgent need to get Saddam to obey the many resolutions it had issued. He cited "flagrant violations" by Saddam towards these resolutions and declared, "We have been more than patient…The conduct of the Iraqi regime is a threat to the authority of the United Nations and a threat to peace." Shortly after the UN speech, the Bush Administration issued a new national security doctrine which justified preemptive military strikes by the United States.

In a speech in Cincinnati in October of 2002, anticipating a congressional vote on a resolution authorizing war against Iraq, Bush explained the need to take military action.

"Some citizens wonder, 'After 11 years of living with this problem, why do we need to confront it now?' And there's a reason. We have experienced the horror of September the 11th. We have seen that those who hate Americans are willing to crash airplanes into buildings full of innocent people. Our enemies would be no less willing, in fact, they would be eager to use biological or chemical or a nuclear weapon. Knowing these realities, America must not ignore the threat gathering among us. Facing clear evidence of peril, we cannot wait for the final proof, the smoking gun that could come in the form of a mushroom cloud."

The President made his case to the American public that we were vulnerable to a terrorist attack, and Iraq was willing to use and to share with terrorist organizations its WMDs. The United States, according to Bush, had no choice but to act decisively to prevent this from happening. The resolution that was passed by the House on October the 10th and by the Senate on the 11th stated:

"The President is authorized to use the Armed Forces of the United States as he determines to be necessary and appropriate, in order to: (1) defend the national security of the United States against the continuing threat posed by Iraq; and (2) enforce all relevant United Nations Security Council resolutions regarding Iraq."

The tally among Congress was as follows; the Democratic leadership, Senate Majority Leader Tom Daschele and House Minority Leader Richard Gephardt both voted in favor of the resolution. The resolution passed in the House by a margin of 296-133. (6 Republicans, 126 Democrats and 1 Independent voted against the measure.) In the Senate, the vote was 77-23 to pass the resolution. (21 Democrats, 1 Republican, and 1 Independent voted against the measure.) Some of the more prominent Democratic Senators that voted in favor of the measure were, Senators Clinton, Biden, Kerry, Feinstein, and Schumer.

The chore now was for Colin Powell to get to work and build a coalition to convince the UN Security Council to pass a new resolution on Iraq. Resolution 144 was a strongly worded and unanimous resolution. It gave Iraq one week to comply with the resolution to inspect weapon sites in

Iraq. The UN inspectors were report back no later than February 21, 2003, on Iraq's compliance. As the UN inspectors searched sites with no visible interference by the Iraqis, by late January they found no "smoking gun," or WMDs. Chief UN Inspector Hans Blix called for more time in order to do a more thorough job. But Bush was growing more and more impatient with the process of inspections. Bush said, "The business about, you know, more time – you know, how much time do we need to see clearly that he's not disarming?....This looks like a rerun of a bad movie, and I'm not interested in watching it." Ahhh, kinda miss Old George, don't cha?

Bush further stated in his State of the Union address on January 28, 2003, that the UN had given Saddam his "final chance to disarm" but "he has shown instead utter contempt for the United Nations and for the opinion of the world." Bush then declares "...the course of the United States does not depend on the decisions of others...We will consult, but let there be no misunderstanding. If Saddam Hussein does not fully disarm for the safety of our people and for the peace of the world, we will lead a coalition to disarm him."

Throughout February and early March of 2003, the U.S., along with Great Britain, continued to build both troop and supply strength in the region in preparations to go to war. Several last- minute peace attempts failed, and finally, on March 17, 2003, Bush declared, "Saddam Hussein and his sons must leave Iraq within the next 48 hours or the United States would commence military against them." Two days later both U.S. and British troops staged a land invasion heading directly to Baghdad. It took about three weeks for the American troops to overtake the city of Baghdad. We now occupied Baghdad, and the Iraqi people were beginning to realize that the brutal dictatorship of Saddam Hussein had seen its end. This was met by jubilation by many and, of course, looting by some. Government buildings, hospitals, libraries, and the Iraqi national museum was some of the targets of looters.

U.S. Forces began to slowly restore order within the city of Baghdad and were there to assist the Iraqis establish some sort of an interim government. President Bush declared the end of combat on May 3, 2003. The president confidently proclaimed from the deck of a U.S. aircraft carrier off the dangerous coast of California (sense the sarcasm) that," In the battle of Iraq, the United States and its allies prevailed." The president goes on to say, "The battle of Iraq is one victory on a war on terror that began on September 11th, 2001, and still goes on….We have removed an ally of al-Qaeda, and cut off a source of terrorist funding."

Bush talked about the futile search by the UN in trying to find Saddam's cache of WMDs. But it seems the US troops also came up empty in their attempts to find the WMDs that brought us into this war. Bush assured the people of the U.S. that the troops would continue their work in finding biological and chemical weapons stored by Saddam. This time he chooses to not mention the nuclear weapons that Saddam was thought to have stored as well. The President's speech had a threefold purpose according to White House officials: (1) to state that the role of U.S. troops was shifting from war to a police function. (Oh yeah, because that worked so well for us in Vietnam!); (2) to signal to allies that it was time to send humanitarian aid; and (3) to signal to the American voters that the President would now shift his attention to domestic issues in preparation of the 2004 elections. There's a re-election to be won! It's all about the votes, baby. They didn't say that, I did.

But of course, questions lingered. After the war the U.S. did continue to search for those damn WMDs. Along with U.S. troops, the U.S. added a 1,200 member Iraqi Survey Group headed by David Kay of the CIA. Their mission was to scour the country for those weapons and report back directly to the President. Their efforts were also futile, and criticism began to pile up toward the administration. Critics began to question whether our President misled us about the presence of WMD in Iraq, and as a result, improperly posed Iraq as an imminent threat to the security and safety of the United States. There were other serious questions about allegations made by the Bush Administration at that time. One was the connection made by Bush between Saddam and the atrocities of 9/11. Another was the assertion that Iraq had nuclear weapons.

Two days after the attacks of 9/11 according to a Time/CNN poll, 78 percent of responders thought that Saddam had a hand in the attacks on the World Trade Center and the Pentagon. The Bush Administration continued with the party line that there was, indeed, a link between Saddam and the al-Qaeda 9/11 hijackers. The problem with this was there was never any solid evidence to back up the claim of such a link between Saddam and al-Qaeda. As hard as the FBI and CIA worked to find a link, none was to be found. No weapons and no link to al-Qaeda. Whoops. It's not until September 18, 2003, that Bush concedes, "No, we've had no evidence that Saddam Hussein was involved in September 11th." No explanation was ever given as to the change in the narrative by the President. Ok, enough. We were lied to, no doubt. My question is, was the President given inaccurate intelligence, or was he knowingly a part of this campaign to wage war against Saddam and Iraq? I would venture a guess that we will never know for sure, or I'll be long gone before accurate info is released. Oh, and by the way, as of the writing of this book in the spring of 2017, although the United States and NATO formally ended its combat mission in Afghanistan on December 28, 2014, U.S. troops are still there. The current death toll for our troops is over 4,500 in Iraq and 2,400 in Afghanistan. The total cost to the American taxpayers is rapidly approaching $5 TRILLION. That's a whole lot of money, folks. But hey, George got his man. Unfair shot at George W. Bush, I'll admit. Although I would like to believe that our President was acting properly on our behalf and to believe in the honesty and integrity of the man, I unfortunately have some very grave doubts. Sorry.

Now on to the Election of 2004. Bush faced little opposition for the Republican nomination. John Kerry, a US Senator from Massachusetts, prevailed in the Democratic nomination process. Since this election would take place only 18 months after the beginning of the Iraq War and three years after the attacks of 9/11, the central focus of this Presidential campaign would be on terrorism and the lack of evidence of Iraq having WMDs. Kerry also touted plans to roll back some of what he called tax cuts for the rich. (really, Richey Rich? As if you didn't take advantage of those cuts? We didn't see you offering to give back cash from those cuts either, did we, Johnny Boy?) Debates over religion, abortion, and gay and civil rights also crept into the discussion. The money spent on the two campaigns was high with both candidates spending well over $300 million. Voter turnout was also high with 60.7 percent turnout or 122 million voters taking to the polls on election night. It was, in fact, the highest voter turnout since the election of 1968. Bush went on to defeat Kerry in a highly contentious and close election. Not Bush vs. Gore close as in 2000, but close nonetheless. The election came down, once again, to one state, but this time, thank God, it's Ohio and not Florida. Bush finished with 50.7 percent of the vote and 286 electoral votes (16 more than the required 270) while Kerry finished with 48.3 percent of the vote and 251 electoral votes. (John Edwards managed to garner one electoral vote.)

George W. Bush entered his second term as president embolden by a larger Republican majority in both the House of Representatives and the Senate. He promised to help with our declining economy, reduce unemployment and lower national debt, along with heading off any domestic security fears. He also promised to privatize Social Security and overhaul the tax system. Oh, and yes, he promised to bring an era of democracy to Iraq.

By mid-decade the economy showed signs of revival, bolstered by the continuing surge in the housing market. Bush, however, faced stiff opposition to his ideas on privatizing Social Security, and it was never presented for a vote. The tide of approval toward the President and the Republican Party as a whole started to turn downward in 2005. A series of ethics-related scandals emerged. Republican House Majority Leader Tom

Delay was forced to step down when a Texas grand jury indicted him on criminal charges that he conspired to violate campaign finance laws. Delay reportedly sought donations to his Political Action Committee from Enron and other corporations to help finance the redistricting of Texas to favor the election of more Republicans. Delay and some of his chief aides were also linked to influence peddling along with lobbyist, Jack Abramoff. Those charges led to imprisonment for both Abramoff and Delay's aides. Delay was eventually convicted in 2010 on his charges. He, of course, appealed the conviction and remained out of prison while he fought this case in court. His conviction was, indeed, overturned in 2013 by a Texas Circuit Court. In 2014 prosecutors appealed to the highest criminal court to reinstate the conviction. The Texas Court of Criminal Appeals eventually upheld the ruling to overturn the conviction in 2016. Delay was now out from under all charges, and he was a free man. While appealing his charges, how did he spend his free time, you ask? Well, like any other washed up celebrity or quasi-celebrity, he made an appearance on *Dancing with the Stars* in 2009. He must have been real worried about his appeal, huh? Thought you might care to know that tidbit.

2006 brought suspicions of national security related government wiretapping along with allegations of torture of some suspected terrorists alarming the civil libertarians among us. 2007 had U.S. Attorney General Alberto Gonzales forced to resign after a probe into the "political" firings of eight U.S. Attorney's. Later that year, Lewis "Scooter" (you already know how I feel about that name) Libby, who was special assistant to Vice-President Dick Cheney, was convicted of lying to a special counsel (special assistant lying to a special counsel…ha) regarding his role in a politically motivated leak of a CIA covert identity, a whole other story to be told in another book at a later time. Libby was sentenced to 30 months in prison for obstructing the investigation of the leak, but before going off to serve his time, President Bush commuted his sentence. He was still liable for the $250,000 fine imposed by the federal court, however. Libby was also disbarred in the District of Columbia in 2008, but he was later reinstated to the D.C. bar in 2016. Libby went to the bar with 11 letters of support from a federal judge and other legal hotshots. In his letter, Judge Lawrence Silberman of the U.S. Court of Appeals for the D.C. Circuit wrote of Libby, "He had a reputation of a skilled and ethical government official." Skilled perhaps, ethical…eh, not so much.

Bush's second term, however, would be defined by an event caused by Mother Nature herself. In late August of 2005, Hurricane Katrina devastated parts of Alabama, Mississippi, Florida, and Louisiana, especially the city of New Orleans. Hurricane Katrina, a Category 3 storm, had sustained winds of over 100 mph and stretched across some 400 miles when it slammed into the Gulf South Coast.

This natural disaster occurred four years after the attacks of 9/11, three years after the creation of the Department of Homeland Security, and one year after that department prepared a National Response Plan. Unfortunately, with all these measures to keep us secure at home, the government response to Hurricane Katrina was a complete failure. As we were all glued to our TV's, watching the destruction the storm laid on the city of New Orleans, government responders seemed unable and ill-prepared to offer the very basic protections needed from the ravages of this storm.

Hurricane Katrina was the largest natural disaster in the U.S. in living memory. The damage was seen over an estimated 92,000 square mile radius. One major city was destroyed as the results of this storm. Over 1,800 people died, and tens of thousands were left homeless and without basic supplies. But with all this, the federal responders somehow failed to see the need to better actively engage in a relief effort on the ground. Many key institutional agencies of every level of government from local to state to federal who were in place to respond to such situations were at fault. The Federal Emergency Management Agency (FEMA) was weakened over the course of Bush's presidency and the newly formed DHS (Department of Homeland Security), an untested organization, was unsure how to deploy its authority and resources. Looking back at the actions or inactions of the DHS, critics feel that they never quite grasped the fact that Katrina was an incident of national significance on par with 9/11. The DHS initially responded as if Katrina was a routine natural disaster until it was just too late. Nothing routine here. In fact, a very complex situation especially in New Orleans.

Not only did the storm wreak havoc on the city, but there was also a collapse of man-made levees meant to protect a city that was built below sea level. A series of problems occurred making Katrina an example of a new type of complex crisis. The crisis was described by Patrick Lagadek, an analyst and international consultant in the field of in-crisis intelligence and leadership in volatile contexts, systematic meltdown situations and unknown territories. Man, we could have used his superpowers here, huh? He stated that, "Katrina caused persistent flooding, a series of industrial disasters, critical evacuation challenges, widespread lethal pollution, the destruction of 90% of the essential utility networks (energy, communications, water etc.), unprecedented public safety concerns, concerns over the possible loss of the port area (which is essential to the continent's economy), even uncertainty as to whether portions of the city could be saved." As I said earlier, nothing routine here. Intelligence of any form was void, and there was a definite absence of effective leadership here.

The sad fact is that the threat of this type of disaster had been known for quite some time. In fact, FEMA, years before the hurricane, ranked the New Orleans situation as one of the most critical potential disasters facing the U.S. Then what the hell happened? I will try to convey the highlights (or lowlights) of the response to Katrina, keeping in mind this is not a comprehensive listing by any means.

Friday August 26ᵗʰ

- Governor Kathleen Blanco declares a state of emergency in Louisiana.

- Gulf Coast states ask for troop assistance from the Pentagon.

Saturday August 27ᵗʰ

- Gov. Haley Barbour declares state of emergency in Mississippi.

- Katrina upgraded to Category 3 Hurricane.

- Gov. Blanco asks Bush to declare a federal state of emergency in Louisiana.

"I have determined that this incident is of such severity and magnitude that effective response is beyond the capabilities of the State and affected local governments and that supplementary Federal assistance is necessary to save lives, protect property, public health, and safety, or to lessen or avert the threat of a disaster." [Office of the Governor]

- Federal emergency declared, DHS and FEMA given full authority to respond to Katrina.

Sunday August 27ᵗʰ

- 9:30 am CDT – Mayor Nagin issues first ever mandatory evacuation of New Orleans.

- Bush, Brown (head of FEMA) and Chertoff (head of DHS) warned of Levee failure by the National Hurricane Center Director.

"We were briefing them way before landfall. ...It's not like this was a surprise. We had in the advisories that the levee could be topped." Director Dr. Mayfield, Director of National Hurricane Center. [Times-Picayune; St Petersburg Times]

- **Approximately 30,000 evacuees gather at the Superdome with roughly 36 hours of food available. [Times-Picayune}**

- **Louisiana National Guard requests 700 buses from FEMA for evacuations.**

FEMA sends 100 buses.

Monday August 29th - Day of the Storm

- **7AM CDT – Katrina makes landfall as a Category 4 hurricane [CNN]**

- **7:30AM CDT – Bush administration notified of the levee breach.**

The administration finds out a levee in New Orleans was breached. On this day 28 *"government agencies from local Louisiana parishes to the White House reported that New Orleans levees were breached."* [AP]

- **Mayor Nagin reports water is flowing over levee.**

- **White House circulates internal memo about levee breach [AP]**

- **Morning presidential briefing where Brown warns Bush about the potential devastation of Katrina.**

Brown warns, *"This is, to put it mildly, the big one, I think."* He voiced concerns that the federal government might not have the capacity to *"respond to a catastrophe within a catastrophe."* He reported to Bush that he felt that the *"Superdome was ill-equipped to be a refuge of last resort."* [AP]

- **Mayfield warns Bush about the topping of the levees.**

- **Bush calls Secretary Chertoff to discuss....wait for it...wait for it....Immigration. Yes, Immigration, not devastation. [White House]**

- **Bush shares birthday cake photo-op with Senator McCain. [White House]**

  Bush visits Arizona resort to promote Medicare Drug Benefit.... yep...Medicare Drug Benefit. [White House]

- **Bush travels to California to promote Medicare Drug Benefit. [White House]**

(Can't make this shit up.)

- **Rumsfeld (Secretary of Defense) – attends San Diego Padres game joined by the team owner in the owner's private box. [Editor and Publisher]**

No better time to see a ballgame than the day of one of our nation's worst natural disaster, huh?

- **8PM CDT – Blanco again requests assistance from Bush.**

  "Mr. President we need your help, we need everything you've got." [Newsweek]

- **Late PM – Bush goes to sleep without acting on Blanco's request.**

Hey, he was tired from all that promoting and flying.

Tuesday August 30th

- **Bush speaks on Iraq at Naval Base Coronado. [White House]**

- **Midday – Chertoff claims he finally became aware that levee had breached.**

Really, buddy? You're gonna claim ignorance here? Reports note that the Bush Administration had learned of the breach on August 29th. [AP]

- **U.S.S. Bataan sits offshore virtually unused.**

"The U.S.S. Bataan, an 844-foot ship designed to dispatch marines in amphibious assaults, has helicopters, doctors, hospital beds, food, and water. It also can make its own water, up to 100,000 gallons a day. And it just so happened to be in the Gulf of Mexico when Katrina came roaring ashore. The Bataan rode out the storm and then followed it toward shore, awaiting relief orders. Helicopter pilots flying from its deck were some of the first to begin plucking stranded New Orleans residents. But now the Bataan's hospital facilities, including six operating rooms and beds for 600 patients, are empty." [Chicago Tribune]

- **2PM CDT – Bush plays guitar with Country singer Mark Willis.**

Yep...not a care in the world. Great optics, Mr. President.

- **Bush returns to Crawford, Texas for his final day of vacation.**

Go ahead. I'll wait... read that again...

Wednesday August 31st

- **FEMA staff warned Brown that people were dying at the Superdome.**

Three hours later Brown's staff gets back to FEMA staff that Brown needs more time to eat his lunch. *"He needs much more than 20 to 30 minutes. We now have traffic to encounter to go to and from a location of his choice followed by wait service from the restaurant staff, eating etc. Thank you."* [AP]

- **National Guard Troops arrive in Louisiana, Mississippi, Alabama and Florida.**

Troops arrive two days after they are requested. [Boston Globe]

- **80,000 believed stranded in New Orleans. 3,000 stranded in the Convention Center without food or water.**

- **Bush surveys damage from Air Force One.**

This was to be the defining moment etched in time for Bush on how he responded (or didn't respond to the disaster). He chooses to fly over the wreckage instead of being on the ground displaying some sort of leadership.

- **Chertoff "Extremely pleased with the response of the government."**

"We are extremely pleased with the response that every element of the federal government has made to this terrible tragedy." [Department of Homeland Security]

Can this guy be that out of touch with reality? This doesn't go over very well, especially for those clinging from rooftops or stranded at the Superdome or the Convention Center.

- **Blanco again tries to request help from Bush.**

"She was transferred around the White House for a while until she ended up on the phone with Fran Townsend, the president's Homeland security advisor, who tried to assure her but did not have many specifics. Hours later. Blanco called back and insisted on speaking to the President. When he came on the line, the governor recalled, "I just asked him for help, whatever you have." She requested 40,000 troops. [Newsweek]

Wow, the Governor of the state under siege by this storm and its aftermath is given the run-around! Despicable, indeed.

- **Bush finally gives an address on Katrina.**

According to reports from the New York Times, *"Nothing about the President's demeanor...which seemed casual to the point of carelessness...suggested that he understood the depth of the current crisis."*

Ok, since I am not a mind reader, I wouldn't know what Bush was thinking or feeling at that moment. But as a leader, you must project and convey a certain message to the people who are waiting for your directions. Acting casual doesn't get that done. Just saying.

- **Secretary of State Condoleezza Rice takes in a Broadway play.**

Coming off a grueling travel schedule, Rice was invited to New York to watch the US Open Tennis Tournament. It was a well-deserved vacation for Rice. However, as the storm hit, perhaps cutting short the outing and heading back to DC would have been a better idea. She was seen at the play and the next day seen shoe shopping at a ritzy NY shop. Bad optics.

- **FEMA Director Brown claims surprise over the size of the storm.**

"I must say, this storm is much bigger than anyone expected." [CNN]

Holy shit, you can't make this up.

Thursday September 1st

- **Bush claims no one expected levees to break.**

I don't know what to say here, and I won't bother to point to the many prior reports indicating the distinct possibility that the levees could break. This statement is indefensible and inexcusable. See August 27th.

- **Still no Command and Control established.**

Terry Ebbert, New Orleans Homeland Security Director had this to say: *"This is a national emergency. This is a national disgrace. FEMA has been here three days, yet there is no command and control. We can send massive amounts of aid to tsunami victims. But we can't bail out the city of New Orleans."* [Fox News]

Can't say I blame him for his frustration. Could you?

- **Michael Brown claims he hasn't heard of any reports pertaining to violence in New Orleans.**

"I've had no reports of unrest, if the connotation of the word unrest means that people are beginning to riot, or you know, banging on walls and screaming and hollering or burning tires or whatever. I've had no reports of that." [CNN]

One word, WOW. Who are these people, and how did they ever get their jobs?

Friday September 2ⁿᵈ

- **Bush staff create a DVD of the week's newscast for the President to view.**

"The reality, say several aides who did not wish to be quoted because it might displease the President, did not really sink in until Thursday night. Some White House staffers were watching the evening news and thought the President needed to see the horrific reports coming out of New Orleans. Counselor Bartlett made up a DVD of the newscasts so Bush could see them in its entirety as he flew down to the Gulf Coast the next morning on Air Force One." [Newsweek]

Storm hits Monday, let's get the President up to speed on this thing on Friday morning. Hey, nothing big, just a little wind and rain and end-of-the-world flooding.

- **Bush praises Mike Brown.**

Yep, you read that right. Bush says in a famous quote from this whole mess,

"Brownie, you're doing a heck of a job!" [White House 9/2/05]

- **Both Bush and FEMA's number 2 express satisfaction with government emergency response.**

- **And this tidbit from our President.**

Remarking on Senator Trent Lott's house, which was damaged by the storm, *"Out of the rubbles of Trent Lott's house...he lost his entire house...there's going to be a fantastic house. And I'm looking forward to sitting on the porch."* Time called the remarks, *"astonishingly tone deaf to the homeless black citizens still trapped in the post-apocalyptic water world of New Orleans."* [White House; Time]

Couldn't say it any better. Move on.

- **Congress approve initial funding of $10.5 billion for rescue and relief aid.**

An additional $51.8 Billion would be quickly allocated to help with the recovery mission.

I'm getting tired of all this incompetency, aren't you? This was one big colossal cluster-fuck, if there ever was one. There is so much more to this, so many instances of continued mismanagement by all levels of government. This would be the beginning of the end for Bush in the eyes of many in the country. Two major events that would go on to define the Bush presidencies, 9/11 and Katrina, both times Bush came up short. I am baffled by the level of unawareness by the President and his staff, many would criticize the President for a lack of leadership and in Katrina's case, lack of compassion. Katrina was mismanaged by everyone involved. As a result of his bungling, FEMA's head, Mike Brown, would be stripped of his relief duties and would eventually step down from his position.

The House of Representatives would go on to release a 600-page report on the handling of Katrina by the White House. It would criticize the President and Chertoff for their actions. By the way, the White House refused to cooperate with any investigations into its handling of Katrina. However, Bush would go on to take responsibility of the failed response. Whew, tough to stomach, huh?

To say that the Bush Administration had its hands full would be an understatement. During its two-term tenure, they had to deal with a mild recession as he took office in 2001, deal with the first attack on U.S. soil since Pearl Harbor, leading him to fund two wars at the same time, then deal with the most damaging hurricane in U.S. history. The final blow was a second recession which would be described many times as the worst since the Great Depression. But what exactly happened to cause this recession and how much blame should the Bush Administration get?

One thing is certain, Bush presided over a widespread failure to regulate. It was during his watch that US authorities allowed the sale of millions of mortgages that people would never be able to afford. It was during his time as President that his Administration failed to police the market on the controversial mortgage-backed securities which eventually collapsed and had devastating consequences. Then there's the credit default swaps, a multibillion dollar bet waged by the banks that other people will go bust, being unregulated as well. Bush's fault? Well, he is the man in charge.

But not all blame is his. Some experts see the repeal of the Glass-Steagall Act as a major cause of the financial crisis in 2008. The Glass-Steagall Act of 1933 separated the activities of commercial banks, which take deposits, from investment banks that invest money. It was repealed in 1999 by Democrat Bill Clinton. The relaxation of these rules allowed commercial lenders such as Citigroup to trade mortgage-backed securities. Bad, bad idea indeed.

It is certainly a noble cause to see everyone own a home. But realistically, homeownership is not a birthright but a hard-earned privilege. By lending people money knowing they will never be able to pay back the loan is both careless and unscrupulous. And for those whose job it is to monitor our economy, shame on them. Reckless lending practices, coupled with the pie-in-the-sky notion that housing prices will perpetually rise was foolhardy. Greed and irresponsibly by lenders and borrowers are to blame as well. The fact of the matter is it all collapsed, and it collapsed with Bush in office. Although he doesn't get all the blame, as Harry S. Truman would say, "the buck stops here!"

Moving forward, very early on in the 2008 election campaign, a Democratic victory seemed likely. George W. Bush had very low approval ratings, and the war in Iraq was widely unpopular. Polls taken early on showed that people felt that the Democrats were better able to handle the problems facing our nation. The results of the 2006 mid-term elections seemed to bear this out as the Democrats were successful in capturing control of Congress. This was seen as another negative byproduct of the Bush Presidency. And let's not forget the cloud of a deteriorating economy that hung over the election as well.

At the start of 2008 many pundits were predicting an easy Clinton victory for the Democratic nomination. She was an experienced Senator with husband, former President Bill Clinton, by her side. He would offer his keen political experiences to guide her as well as his prodigious fundraising skills to get the money needed to fund a successful primary season. Her main opponents were seen as Senator Barak Obama (Ill.) and John Edwards, former Senator (N.C.), who also campaigned in the 2004 primaries. Obama was first seen to be too inexperienced and a bit out of his depth, while Edwards was openly criticized for announcing his candidacy while his wife battled cancer, although she supported his run. Edwards would eventually have other problems such as an extra-marital affair which led to a child and federal charges of improper campaign finances.

Late 2007, Clinton was ahead by as much as 20 points in a number of reputable polls over Senator Obama. The first real test for Clinton would come at the caucus held in Iowa in January 2008. Many were expecting that this would be Clinton's first steps toward the Democratic nomination. Oops. Didn't go as planned, folks. Not only did she lose to Obama, she was pushed to third by Edwards. Didn't see that coming, huh, Hillary? So, what happened in Iowa? Well to begin with, Iowa has never elected a woman to any position of authority before, and it seems it wasn't going to start here either. She lost the young vote and the black vote by a wide margin. It is that margin (72% to 16%) that is disturbing because Clinton was associated in her early career with the civil rights movement in the south. Another misstep by Clinton was aligning herself with older former cabinet members such as Madeleine Albright former Secretary of State, and General Wesley Clark, former head of NATO. Many saw this as attaching herself to the past and having no vision for the future. Meanwhile, Obama was seen as the younger-more-attuned-to-the future candidate. In his stump speeches, he frequently referred to the future of the U.S., and apparently, it was the message that voters wanted to hear.

Many called this defeat in Iowa an embarrassment for Clinton, and it certainly was not the way Clinton wanted to kick off the primary season. To show how fickle our media can be, many areas of the media started to write her off as a result of her defeat in Iowa. Remember Iowa was the FIRST primary in a long season of primaries. Next up was New Hampshire and predictably all the polls had Obama winning. So what happens? Clinton wins and the fickle press now refers to her as the "comeback gal". Clinton was able to capitalize on the women's as well as the low-income voters in New Hampshire. The victory caught Clinton supporters and her campaign team by surprise. This is the way the primary season progressed, swings back and forth from one candidate to the other. Edwards by this time dropped out so it narrowed the choice to Obama or Clinton. Even "Super Tuesday" and its over 2,000 delegates couldn't decide the nomination. The contest would rage on into June with the last two primaries in South Dakota and Montana. When the dust settled, it was Obama with the number of delegates needed to win the nomination. He needed 2,118 delegates, and by June 4th he had 2,181. Clinton would settle with 1,919 delegates. It was a highly contested and at times contentious contest between two unique candidates. On June 7th, Clinton officially conceded and promised her full support for Obama in his campaign against the Republican opponent, Senator John McCain (AZ).

John McCain's road to the Republican nomination was a bit easier than Obama's. McCain was a war hero who was seen by many to have the ability to reach across the aisle, therefore offering a better option to American voters. As early favorites such as Rudy Giuliani faded from consideration, it became a race between McCain, Mitt Romney former Governor from Massachusetts, Mike Huckabee former Governor from Arkansas, and dark-horse candidate Ron Paul. As the primary season progressed, it was apparent that McCain was the strong favorite. Mike Huckabee was the last to concede in March 2008, and McCain became the Republican candidate for President. This allowed McCain the time to formulate a game plan in hopes of defeating the eventual Democratic candidate Barack Obama.

With McCain claiming victory earlier than Obama, and Obama in a death match with Clinton, the Republicans were polling better than the Democrats through the spring of 2008. It's not until Obama clinches the nomination in June that the Democrats reassert themselves in the race for the Presidency. Both candidates would run on a platform of change and reform in Washington (seems they always do, right?).

With few exceptions, Obama repeatedly polled higher than McCain throughout the campaign. Obama would chose as his running mate Senator Joe Biden (DE), a career politician. Biden is the former chairman of the Senate Committee on Foreign Relations, which was thought to compensate for Obama's inexperience abroad. Biden is also nineteen years Obama's senior, bolstering the image of a young and inexperienced Obama. On the other hand, McCain's pick for a running mate was highly questionable, Governor Sarah Palin of Alaska. Although she was younger and offset McCain's age (he would have been the oldest person elected to a first-term as President), she was also extremely inexperienced for the national and international stage. Many things have been said and written about Palin as McCain's choice for V.P., some good, most bad. The fact was, McCain wasn't going to win this race with or without her. Many critics use revisionist history when discussing Palin. Fact was most of the negative feedback concerning Palin were revealed after the race. Sure, there were some unfortunate and damaging moments where Palin showed an astonishing lack of knowledge in both domestic and foreign affairs. Her TV interviews with Charles Gibson and especially Katie Couric were both eye-opening and at times laughable. But the facts show that after naming her as his running mate, there was a spike of support for the Republican ticket, and at the beginning of the race, Palin had an 81% approval rating.

Nevertheless it was a resounding victory for Barack Obama. Obama would garner over 66 million votes compared to 58 million for McCain. He also won a decisive margin in the Electoral College, 365-173. President Obama would be the first African-American elected president! It would also signal a return to the Democratic Party calling the shots in the White House. This is after eight years of George W. Bush and the Republican Party having control.

When President Obama does indeed take office in January 2009, he was faced with dire economic circumstances. He would repeatedly refer to it as the worst economic recession since the Great Depression. And he was right! He would also say that it was a mess that he inherited not created. That would also be correct. But hey, he did seek this office, so what was he going to do? And how fast can he get Congress to provide some relief in this recession? The American Recovery and Reinvestment Act was Obama's initial economic stimulus package. Congress approved the $787 BILLION plan in February 2009, one month after the inauguration. Fast enough for ya? The initial purpose was to end the 2008 recession by spurring consumer spending and saving anywhere between 900,000 to over 2 million jobs. Well, that was the plan anyway. Many felt the most important benefit was rebuilding the confidence needed to boost economic growth. The package also aimed to regain trust in the financial industry by limiting bonuses for senior executives in any company that accepted TARP funds, a bill passed by Congress in October 2008 to bail out the banks.

Here's how the American Recovery and Reinvestment Act (ARRA) worked. It was set up with three spending categories. It would cut taxes by$288 billion. It would spend $224 billion in extended unemployment benefits, education, and healthcare. It would also create jobs by allocating $275 billion in federal contracts, grants, and loans. Do the math, I did, that's $787 BILLION. ARRA was set up as a ten-year package, but over 90% would be spent in the first three years. $185 billion for 2009, $400 billion for 2010, and $135 billion for 2011. ARRA actually performed better than planned. By the end of 2009, $241.9 billion had been spent. $92.8 in tax relief, $86.5 billion in unemployment and other benefits, and $62.6 in job creation grants. The money was definitely flowing. In fact, in 2012 Congress allocated additional funds to raise the total under ARRA to $840 billion. By December 2013 $816.3 of that total was already spent. $290.7 in tax relief, $264.4 in benefits, and $261.2 in contracts, grants, and loans.

All these figures are fine and dandy, but did it work? As I discussed in the prior chapter, it didn't seem to do much for me and the many millions of the working middle class. I guess you can sum it up by saying that it didn't necessarily make things better, but it helped to make things less worse. Huh? Think of it this way, ARRA didn't make life better, but without it, life would have been worse. Small victories to say the least.

March 23, 2010, President Obama signed the highly controversial Patient Protection and Affordable Care Act, a 906-page health care reform law that would become known as Obamacare. It took the president a full year of wrangling with Congress to put this bill into law. That's with a Democratic majority that Obama enjoyed in both the House and the Senate for the first two years in office. His focus on this issue amid a deep recession and crippling job losses, was seen as a threat to his reelection chances. Along with the Democratic majorities in both the House and the Senate. It would hurt the partisanship that Obama had hoped to tame during his time in office. The fact that the bill passed through both Houses without receiving a **single** Republican vote points to a widening divide within Congress. The only bipartisanship in this whole mess was in the NO vote as 34 Democrats joined all of the Republicans in fighting against the bill. Obama might have won the battle, but he would eventually lose the war. The broad strokes of the bill expanded coverage to an additional 32 million people and contained spiraling healthcare costs. The battle to improve America's healthcare system is one that dates all the way back to the Teddy Roosevelt presidency at the turn of the 20th century. The prior system worked for the approximately 150 million Americans who are provided health insurance through their employer. But the system fell short when dealing with people who work part-time, are self-employed, or worked for companies and small businesses that did not offer health insurance.

Attached to Obamacare and subsequently passed by the Democratic Congress and signed into law by the president on March 30, 2010, was the Health Care and Education Reconciliation Act. This historic, but less publicized piece of legislation, would end the process of the federal government giving subsidies to private banks to hand out federally insured loans. Instead, future loans would be administered directly by the Department of Education. This amounted to a revolution on how America finances higher education and was overshadowed by the hoopla over Obamacare.

The Obama presidency would be defined by several policies, with Obamacare right at the top. There were many misconceptions about the plan. When viewing the early returns, there's just a lot of misinformation. The idea that Obamacare was causing healthcare costs to rise was just plain false. Fact is that healthcare costs were rising just like all other basic necessities such as, housing, transportation, and education. Healthcare costs had been rising well before Obama took office to the tune of 4.8% per year from 2005-2010. Did costs rise after Obamacare? Yes, it did, but at a lower level of 3.8% per year. So, when critics railed against Obamacare saying costs had risen, they were correct. But they failed to mention that Obamacare had decreased the rising costs by 1% per year over time. The water was, indeed, rising folks. It's just rose at a slower rate. Doesn't mean you're not going to drown. Just means it's gonna take longer for you to see the water rise over your head. Note the cynicism!

Another myth about Obamacare was that it was actually socialized medicine. A concept that has severe connotations in our country. In many respects, they are right. Obamacare can be seen as healthcare that is "one size fits all" or the definition of socialized medicine. Critics of socialized medicine and Obamacare say that not all people have the same healthcare needs. But Obamacare says all must pay so that some can have benefits they otherwise would not be able to afford. This when broken down, is the essence of socialized medicine. For instance, a family that has undergone a permanent contraceptive procedure cannot opt out of family planning or maternity benefits to lower their premiums. One size fits all. People who don't use drugs or abuse alcohol cannot opt out of chemical or alcohol treatments centers in exchange for lower premiums. One size fits all. Men cannot opt out of maternity benefits for lower premiums either. That money might be needed by someone else to use for their maternity needs. Well folks, that's socialized medicine. Just because our doctors for the most part are private and are not federal employees, as in the case of socialized countries such as the U.K. and Canada, doesn't mean it's not in some sense socialized.

Let me take you through what I see as some of the pros and cons of Obamacare, Slatest style. Children under 19 are guaranteed insurable under AHA. This allows parents to provide preventative care for their children. Also the age that children can be kept under a parent's plan has increased from 24 to 26 under Obamacare. Both pros, no? Insurance companies cannot deny coverage due to a preexisting condition. Another check in the pro column. There is no longer a lifetime limit for coverage, free wellness and preventive doctor visits. Pro side, check, check and check. Now for the cons. What's with this tax penalty concept, huh? A penalty of about 2.5-3 percent of your income for choosing no healthcare. Don't like it. Big check in con column. With healthcare now becoming more affordable for all, some will have to pay more. That group includes the high earner and healthcare industries. Well, reluctantly I put this in the con column. I have no love for the top 1% and the healthcare industry as a whole. Oh, the hell with them, I'M now putting this in the pro side. Some smaller companies have decided to forgo offering insurance to their employees. The thinking here is that the penalties imposed for not offering insurance is lower than the cost of insuring their employees. And small businesses feel that their employees would get a better deal on the healthcare market set up by Obamacare. This is a con for me. And with more people lining up for care, will the wait for care increase, and/or will the level of care decrease to meet the increased demand. Hmm, don't know. Have to put this in the con column. This is just some of the issues concerning Obamacare.

I think the best way to view the Obama presidency is to look at the ways America has changed during his tenure. When measuring public opinion over his years as president, we see significant changes in key areas such the economy, race relations, and in the way the public views our government as a whole.

When taking a look at America's views on government, we see that in general people are losing faith in all aspects of our government. We see this when it comes to our elected leaders, to our established institutions, and the agencies that are put in place to provide services to our citizens. The public's faith in our elected leaders shrunk from 49% in 2009 to 42% in Obama's final year. Confidence in the vaunted Supreme Court shrunk during the Obama years as well. In 2014, it hit a record low of 30%. In 2014, Congress reached its nadir with an approval rating of a whopping 7%. But, hey, folks, the majority of us put them there. 7%? Here's a suggestion, get off your butts and vote. 93% don't approve, but yet during the 2014 mid-term election only 36.4% of eligible voters turned out to vote. Come on, folks, don't disapprove then stay home. 2018 is a midterm election, if you don't approve of who's in office or don't approve of the job they are doing, don't complain, vote! Simple concept. "Oh, nobody listens to me" whah! You're right, ELECTED officials only listen to those that ELECT them. If you stay home, it's a self-fulfilling prophecy, ELECTED officials will not listen to you! Enough. Moving on.

Obama's average approval rating from Jan 20, 2009 to Jan 19, 2017 was 47.9%. Since World War II, this places him higher than only three other presidents, Ford, Carter and Truman. Nixon and GW Bush scored higher. Nixon? Wow. Obama started out high with approval ratings in the high 60's and ended high with a final approval rating of 59%. So, I guess the American public was almost as happy to see him leave as they were to see him arrive. Sorry, had to. Too easy to let go. On the plus side, Obama never really had too many swings in his approval ratings. He was consistently mediocre as far as his ratings are concerned. He had a 31-point range between his high and low mark, only Kennedy had a smaller range at 27 points.

Although Obama campaigned in 2008 on the platform of establishing bipartisanship, the president turned out to be very polarizing. The difference in his job approval ratings between Democrats and Republicans was the widest in Gallup polling history. But to be fair, this seems to be a trend since Obama's predecessor, George W. Bush, had the second widest margin. Mistrust it seems, is not just held for our elected officials. Polling indicates that it extends to the electorate as well. In 2009, 73% had trust and confidence in their fellow Americans when making decisions in our democracy. That figure plunged to 56% in 2016. We don't trust elected officials, and we don't trust our fellow Americans when making those decisions. Obama, in his Farewell Address, talked about his regret in failing to reduce the divisiveness that has continued to define American politics. He seemed to be well aware of the problem as he first entered office in 2009, but unfortunately, he was unable to provide a solution.

During the Obama years, there was an increase of Americans who identified themselves as liberal on social issues. At the start of the Obama presidency, about 25% of Americans saw themselves as liberal on social issues. This was in line with the percentage seen in prior years. However, by 2016 almost a third (32%) identified themselves a socially liberal, the highest mark since Gallop started asking this question in 1999. The two social issues where changes were seen the most were in gay marriages and the legal use of marijuana. In 2009, only 40% of Americans were in favor of legal gay marriages. 57% (including President Obama) were opposed. By 2016, after the historic ruling made by the Supreme Court to legalize gay marriages, a robust majority of 61% felt gay marriages should be legal throughout the United States. By Obama's last year in office, over 60% (a record high, no pun intended. Yes, it was) endorsed the legalization of marijuana in the United States. This was compared to the 2009 mark of 44%. Among Democrats, support for legalizing marijuana almost doubled during the Obama years. Other issues that became more "morally acceptable" to Americans were the issues of divorce, sex between unmarried men and women, having a baby outside of marriage, and gay and lesbian relations. Whether this is a direct relation to President Obama or not, the fact remains that in general Americans loosened their views on several social issues.

When looking at President Obama's report card on the how he handled the economy, most fair-minded people would give him a favorable mark. Obama's policies helped lift the economy out of one of its biggest slumps outside of the Great Depression. The scale of the financial crisis we faced in 2008 and the extent of the job losses seen in the beginning of 2009 should never be forgotten. Declines during the first year of the Great Recession (2008-09), especially in areas such as household wealth and employment, were sharper than those seen at the outset of the Great Depression in 1929-30. But despite improvements made in these areas during the Obama years, the U.S. economy still faces the same challenges that were present as when Obama took office. We still face competition from countries who offer low-wages jobs, a real short-fall in productivity growth, and the alarmingly high levels of income equality. All of which were discussed earlier. Certainly not the fault of President Obama entirely, but critics would say nothing was achieved by Obama's policies in trying to correct this situation. Although it's a truism among economists that presidents get too much blame when the economy is doing badly and too much credit when things are going well, Presidents are not mere bystanders. Their policies in conjunction with Congress matter a great deal. Look no further than the legacies of FDR or Ronald Reagan if you have doubts about a President's effect on a struggling economy.

The one area within our society that causes me the most discomfort when discussing is the deterioration of race relations during the Obama years. Ironic that during the years of our first African-American President, the issues of racial disparities are more evident. "America is a place where all things are possible" was the statement made by Barack Obama the night he was elected as the first black man to be President of the United States in 2008. His tone changes decidedly in his farewell address in 2017 when he says, "Race remains a potent and often a divisive force in our society." It is disappointing to me that President Obama and our country missed an opportunity to make real positive changes on the issue of race relations in America. Both of Obama's statements ring true for me. America is a place where all things are possible, and race is a potent and divisive force in our society today.

Some Americans had hoped that the symbolic moment of a black man getting elected President would usher in a new post-racial era in our country. Others, including the President, saw this as naïve. They pointed to the fact that it takes years and years for change to happen within a society. What's disappointing, though, is the fact that we are not moving any closer towards racial harmony, but we are in fact moving further away from that ever happening in my lifetime. Six months into his first term there was an incident between a black Harvard Professor and a white Cambridge police officer. Professor Henry Louis Gates Jr. was arrested on his front porch after a 9-1-1 call came in saying two black men looked to be breaking into a house. When Sgt. Crowley of the Cambridge Police arrived at the scene he confronted Gates, and depending on whose version you listen to, either Crowley acted in a racist manner or Gates acted in an uncooperative manner. Regardless, when President Obama was asked about the incident during a White House press conference, he replied that the police "acted stupidly." He made this statement before he had received any official account of the matter. This was seen by many, including law enforcement, as the beginning of the divide which would only got wider as his two terms progressed. I will examine the relationship between law enforcement and the communities they serve in my next chapter. The Obama Presidency did not eradicate racial discord but instead illuminated the deep-seeded feelings within both sides of the discord. Each side was equally outraged over the perceived slights they faced. Disappointing, indeed. Perhaps we expected too much. Obviously much more work is needed to address this widening rift.

Now on to the military and foreign policy during the Obama Presidency. Barack Obama, the candidate in 2008, campaigned on a promise to end the wars in both Iraq and Afghanistan. During his second term, he promised to lift the U.S. from what he called a permanent war footing. But in reality, President Obama left a very different legacy when he exited the office in January 2017. He was the first two-term president to be at war throughout his entire tenure. Under his command, the U.S. launched airstrikes or raids into seven different countries: Afghanistan, Iraq, Syria, Libya, Yemen, Somalia, and Pakistan. According to U.S. Intelligence, the U.S. faces more threats, in more places, than at any time since the Cold War. Some experts feel that we have also revived potential threats from our most potent adversaries, Russia and China.

During the Obama Presidency, the number of U.S. troops in war zones were dramatically decreased from 150,000 to 14,000. He stemmed the flow of U.S. body bags returning from war during his tenure. He expanded what is now known as modern warfare by increasing the number of elite commando units and introducing modern technology, employing armed drones and cyber weapons. President Obama chose to use diplomacy at times, avoiding warfare in such places as Iran during a nuclear standoff between our nations.

The Obama Administration built various secret drone bases throughout Africa and the Middle East to implement their new strategy. The administration also repositioned more troops and warships into the western Pacific as well as move both troops and equipment into Eastern Europe to counter a resurgent Russian presence in the region. There were many instances when the Obama Administration would clash with its top military advisors. Three former Secretaries of Defense (Panetta, Hagel and Gates) accused the White House and Obama directly of micromanaging the military.

Circumstances found Obama president during a time known as the Arab-Spring uprisings'. These uprisings occurred throughout the Middle East and North Africa in 2011. During one of these uprisings, Obama reluctantly approved a NATO plan for airstrikes in Libya aimed to stop the slaughter of innocent civilians by its leader, Moammar Kaddafi. Obama wanted to avoid any prolonged presence in Libya, trying to avoid another situation like the one in Iraq. The U.S left Libya after Kaddafi was killed leading the country to collapse in conflict and also created a dangerous vacuum for terrorist groups to rise in this oil-rich country. One such terror group known as Ansar al Sharia would rise and lead an attack on a U.S. Diplomatic compound and CIA base in Benghazi, Eastern Libya, on September 11, 2012. The attack resulted in the death of U.S. Ambassador J. Christopher Steven along with three other Americans. The attack would lead to many unanswered questions for the people within the Obama Administration, and in particular, Hillary Clinton, who was the then Secretary of State.

The first serious question was: Did the Obama administration knowingly mislead the American public with initial claims that the attack was a spontaneous response to an anti-Muslim video that appeared on YouTube? Government e-mails would surface shortly after the attacks indicating that both the White House and the State Department were told as the attacks were occurring in real-time, that Ansar al Sharia, then a little-known terrorist group, was taking credit for the attacks. What was not known was why did the administration continue to offer the story of a spontaneous response to an anti-Muslim video, and only slowly come to acknowledge that this was a premediated terror attack on our compounds?

The fallout from Benghazi would extend to the 2016 Presidential Election with Hillary Clinton, the Democratic candidate, a key figure in this mess. Her critics used the handling of this matter as an example of her inability to deliver decisive leadership solutions in a critical moment. The crux of an exhaustive report released by House Republicans in 2016 was aimed at both Clinton and Obama for promoting the false narrative of a spontaneous reaction to a video. Clinton had in fact sent an e-mail to her daughter on the night of the attacks, stating that an al-Qaeda faction was responsible for the attacks. Many felt that the narrative presented by Clinton and Obama was an attempt to deflect any criticism of how inadequately protected the compounds were. Especially after threat assessments were presented indicating this was a highly volatile area, and the U.S. should have considered pulling stakes prior to the attacks.

On to the next mess. Many feel that Obama and his administration will be forever stained by its response, or lack thereof, to the chaos and carnage that also occurred in Syria. With over a half million dead since the March 2011 uprising that sparked war, many in the foreign policy community felt that Obama could have done much more in terms of military support. Debatable at best. The facts are as follows, the Syrian conflict is in its seventh year, 500,000 dead, more than a million injured, and well over 12 million Syrians, half of its prewar population - displaced from their homes. In 2011 in what became known as the Arab Spring, revolts toppled the Presidents of both Tunisia and Egypt. In March of 2011, peaceful protests surfaced in Syria in response to 15 young boys being beaten and tortured for writing graffiti in support of the Arab Spring. The Syrian government and its President, Bashar al-Assad, responded to the protests by killing hundreds of demonstrators and imprisoning many more. As a response to the brutal government actions, defectors from the Syrian military announced the formation of the Free Syrian Army. Its purpose was to overthrow Assad and his government, starting a very brutal civil war.

In what started out as a civil war, has become a very complex international situation. The best way to decipher who's fighting whom in this war, is to think along the lines of who supports Assad and the Syrian government, and who opposes Assad and his government. Those who support Assad are: (a) **Russia** (provides political support for Syria at the UN and also carries out air-strikes) (b) **Iran** (provides arms, credit, advisors and some say military troops) (c) **Hezbollah**- Lebanese Shia movement (has sent thousands of troops) (d) **Shia Muslim militias** (recruited by Iran from Iraq, Afghanistan and Yemen).

On the rebel side are: (a) **Turkey** (provides arms, military and political support) Gulf Arab States (provides money and weapons) (b) The **U.S.** (provides arms, training and military assistance to "moderate rebel groups" (c) **Jordan** (logistical support and training)

And then there is **ISIS,** or Islamic State in Iraq, and al-Sham/the Levant. ISIS saw an opportunity in Syria with all the surrounding chaos to carve out a large portion of the country for their "caliphate," which they created several years before. Both sides are fighting them, not together, but in two separate anti-ISIS factions. Everyone hates ISIS it seems. While supporters and resisters of Assad fight against one another, both sides fight against ISIS. Nothing is easy in the Middle-East, which is why Obama was reluctant to get the U.S. involved all along. Oh, wait, I forgot the **Kurds**. Kurdish people who live in Northern Syria which was declared an autonomous government in areas they controlled in early 2014. The Kurds say they have no side in the Syrian war, but they too hate ISIS and are battling them along the Turkish border. The Kurds however, have benefitted most from the U.S. by supplying the Kurds with military support in their fight against ISIS. The U.S. see the Kurds as the most effective anti-ISIS force on the ground.

Just how did all this international involvement come about? Let's start with Russia. Russia has military interests in Syria, namely its only Mediterranean naval base and an airbase in the Latakia province. Although it intervened at the request of President Assad, Russia and its leader, Vladimir Putin, say its motivation for getting involved is solely to fight terrorism. Cynics would say Russia is hoping to bolster its presence in the Middle East and throughout the world by getting involved in Syria. Next is Iran. They see Assad as its closest Arab ally, and coincidentally, Syria just happens to be the main transit point for weapons going between Iran and Hezbollah in Lebanon.

On the rebel side, The Gulf States, mainly Saudi Arabia, are predominantly Sunni Muslim. They are opposed to the predominantly Shia population of Iran's influence in Syria. In case you didn't know, Shia Muslims and Sunni Muslim have had a "problem" with each other for centuries. Really, centuries. Look it up. It's complicated. The U.S. got involved in backing the rebel groups when it said Assad was responsible for widespread atrocities in Syria.

The instance that would define Obama's legacy in this affair came when he declared in 2012 that the use of chemical weapons by Assad and Syria would be crossing a "red line" that would require American military involvement. Assad a year later defied and perhaps called Obama out by firing rockets filled with sarin gas into towns around Damascus which killed an estimated 1,400 civilians. On September 13, 2013, Obama addressed our nation. He urged for U.S. intervention in Syria, saying that it would be in the best interests of both our country and the entire world. He went on to say in his address;

"If we fail to act, the Assad regime will see no reason to stop using chemical weapons...As the ban against these weapons erode, other tyrants will have no reason to think twice about acquiring poison gas and using them. Over time our troops would again face the prospect of chemical weapons on the battlefield, and it could be easier for terrorist organizations to obtain these weapons and use them to attack civilians."

When Obama went to Congress, he was met with little enthusiasm in getting involved in Syria at that time. Obama would then back down from his threat to Assad and allowed Russia and Putin to spearhead the solution of chemical weapons being used by the Assad regime. The Russians said that Syria agreed to dismantle its chemical weapons stockpile in exchange for escaping any punishment for war crimes committed by the regime. By 2015, Obama felt confident that Syria had abandoned its chemical weapons. But subsequent chemical attacks by Syria took place in April 2017 after Obama left office. This time our current president, Donald Trump, took action by bombing Syrian airfields. Trump did this without waiting for any Congressional approval unlike his predecessor. Obama's weak "red line" threat and the handing off to Russia the task of dismantling Syria of its chemical weapons served to unleash a torrent of Syrian refugees throughout Europe. It also allowed for the reemergence of Russia on the world stage, and it left the real possibility of terrorists getting their hands on chemical weapons. Not what you would call a shining moment for Barack Obama and his administration.

The Obama foreign policy, when looked upon with non-biased appraisal, was somewhat lacking. There were some victories along the way, but there were more major defeats. One way to judge his policies is to look at how the U.S. stands throughout the world as he exited office. We stand weaker now than when Obama first entered the presidency. How so, you might ask? By the end of the Obama presidency, can you think of an area in the world where the U.S. is in a stronger position than when he first entered the White House? Anywhere? Our allies have lost confidence in us, and our enemies have less fear. Look around the world, are any countries more free or friendlier as a result of Obama policies? But to be fair, let's look at some of his victories. The Obama Administration did manage to negotiate a deal with Iran to limit their nuclear capabilities. He followed through on George W. Bush's plan to withdraw troops from Iraq and to reduce our role in Afghanistan. Very importantly, Osama Bin Laden was found and eliminated on Obama's watch. And throughout his presidency, Obama handled himself with dignity, grace, and class. I suspect more people will appreciate this style more as the years of President Trump wear on. But a president isn't judged solely by their style, they are judged more on their results.

Our relationships with traditional allies such as Israel and Saudi Arabia were weaker as a result of Obama's foreign policies. Moscow has asserted its power increasingly in Syria and throughout Eastern Europe. The U.S. relationships in Western Europe have also been called into question as Obama was leaving office.

One area that took a nosedive during the Obama presidency is the number of Democratic officials in our government. In State Houses throughout the country, the Democrats lost 717 seats during the Obama tenure. In State Senates, the number lost is 231. In the U.S. House of Representatives Democrats lost 63 Seats during Obama presidency as well as 12 seats in the U.S. Senate. Add to this the loss of 12 Democratic Governorships during his tenure as well. It's becomes clear that the voters of our country were dissatisfied with the policies of the Obama Administration and looked for a change away from the Democratic Party.

CHAPTER FOUR

Law Enforcement
and Our Communities

ull disclosure here people, I am the son of a NYPD Police Officer. My dad patrolled the streets of Washington Heights in northern Manhattan during the 1960's and '70's. This was a time of change and turbulence in our city. My dad, a Caucasian, walked the streets filled with newly arrived immigrants, most coming from the Dominican Republic. The area became one of poverty and crime, followed by massive drug use and distribution. During his time in the 34th precinct, he never once used his gun or had any allegations of police brutality. He took great pride in his work and loved the area he patrolled. It was also the area he was born and raised and went to school in. My grandmother would stay in that neighborhood for many years after the transformation. It was home. My dad witnessed the racial transformation that took place during that time. It didn't matter to him. What mattered were the hardworking people trying to provide for their families, and he would do anything to protect them. Why am I saying this? Because deep down I believe with all my heart and soul that the great majority of the brave men and women who risk their lives to provide us with safe streets are the same as my dad. Good people doing a very difficult job.

Of course, things have changed from the 1960's, but have they really? Today we are confronted with media reports of a racist police force in our country. There are many incidents of police killing unarmed black men that fill our television sets. Many protests turning violent from a perceived viewpoint that the police are out to kill. It has served only to pit one side against the other: Law enforcement vs. the residents that they serve. From New York to Baltimore to Chicago, from Dallas to Ferguson, one incident after the other where violence has broken out over race vs law enforcement. The Police have become the enemy for many in our cities. But I would like to take a step back and look at our Law Enforcement agencies and also look at our cities and the people with the loudest voices of opposition towards our police. Let's put rhetoric and grandstanding aside. I'm not here to blindly support law enforcement, but to try to look at the numbers and the facts as we know them. Warts will appear, no system is perfect. Our police forces are being asked to do much more than they have in the past. Somewhere along the line it has become the responsibility of our police to solve our more vexing social problems. Problems such as homelessness, drug use and mental illness are now handled by our police who are trained to enforce compliance, not offer therapy.

Many feel we have a racist police problem in our country. They point to Michael Brown in Ferguson, Missouri; Freddie Gray in Baltimore, Maryland; Eric Garner in New York; and Tamir Rice in Cleveland, Ohio, as well as others. They question what is happening in America between unarmed black men and our police? Groups of Americans are quick to jump at the very simplistic response that the police are racist. It's easier to think that it's all the fault of racist police, it is much harder to examine the levels of violence in our country alongside our racism problem and our policing problem. Sometimes the three come together and create one big bloody mess. To treat each separately (violence, racism and policing) might be more productive than to just bundle them all under the guise of a racist police force here in America.

Violence – There is no denying that America is one violent country. The murder rate in our big cities continue to climb. We had over 15,000 gun related murders along with over a million more violent crimes committed in the U.S. in 2016. Nearly 70% of all murders are carried out by firearms, which shouldn't be surprising since it is estimated that America is home to nearly 300 million firearms. It is estimated that the U.S. possesses anywhere from 35-50% of all the firearms worldwide. When compared to other developed countries the sheer scale of violence in America becomes clearer. For example, gun ownership in Great Britain is 6.6 per 100 people; in Germany and France it's 30 per 100; here in the U.S. it's between 88-112 guns per 100 people. Gun homicide rates here in the U.S. are startling. It is three times higher than the rate in France; four times higher than Great Britain; five times more than Germany and a whopping thirteen times more than in Japan.

So let's look inside the numbers here in the United States, shall we? I don't want to cloud the discussion by comparing it to other countries. I care only how violence affects me, and since I live in the U.S., let's just focus here. Good for you? I also don't want this to become a debate over gun ownership. God knows there is plenty to debate. I want to look at the numbers so we can see how one side of the triangle, (violence, racism, policing) play's a huge role in how law enforcement polices our communities. In 2016 according to Gun Violence Archive, (a non-profit corporation formed in 2013 to provide free online public access to accurate information about gun related violence in the United States) there were 15,057 gun related deaths in the U.S. and over 30,600 gun related injuries. From 2005-2015 71 Americans were killed in terror attacks on U.S. soil. During that same time period 301,797 were killed by gun violence on U.S. soil. Mass shootings, as measured as four or more people shot regardless of total fatalities, took place in over 100 metropolitan areas in 2015. As sensational as these occurrences are, they account for less than 2% of all gun deaths. We are talking on the average that 36 Americans per day are killed by a gun, and this excludes suicides. Of these 36 Americans killed each day, roughly 50% of those killed are black men even though they comprise only 6% of the total population here in the U.S. Since these men predominantly come from poor segregated neighborhoods with very little political clout, such killings don't capture America's attention. Here's one for ya, in 2015, on average, a toddler, A TODDLER, shoots someone about once a week. I'll let that sink in for a bit. … This is frightening, less than 10% of all firearms stolen in the U.S. are ever recovered.

Congress which has held 25 moments of silence since the Sandy Hook Elementary School shooting (December 14, 2012) but it has yet to approve a single gun safety bill. Not one. Homicide is the second leading cause of death among all 15-24 year olds and is the leading cause of death for blacks in that age group. Firearm related injuries and deaths have become an important public health concern here in the U.S. The Supreme Court of the United States has clearly supported the right of the individual to bear arms, so we need to start focusing our attention on how to live in a country with so many guns. We are in need of more policies which focus on the reduction of risks and the frequency of gunshot injuries and deaths. Here are some suggestions:

- Universal background checks for all firearm transactions including, private, internet and gun show sales. Also make the needed improvements in our National Instant Criminal Background Check System. (NICS)

- Support all efforts to limit access to firearms by kids by strengthening the laws concerning gunlocks and safe storage techniques, also hold the parents responsible for the consequences of a child accessing and using a firearm.

- Improve the availability and quality of mental health services for those in need. Provide funds for teachers, health care professionals and social workers to help identify those with mental illnesses. Funds for the coordination of facilitating interaction between schools, law enforcement and mental health facilities. Let's start to reduce the stigma attached to those seeking mental health services while we are at it.

- Eliminate language from a Congressional appropriations bill of 1996 that restricts funding of firearms-related research. What are we afraid to find?

- Support limits to high-capacity magazines and assault-type weaponry.

Granted this is barely a start. The crux of the matter goes much deeper. What's going on in our communities that evokes such violence and necessitates police involvement? The police and our communities are at a crisis point. Guns on the streets, mixed with drugs, poverty and broken homes and dreams. Decaying schools and family structures. Young men with no options that will produce positive results. But of course there are exceptions. We have all seen the stories. Let's face facts, for many in our inner cities the picture is bleak indeed. This is the environment that we ask our police to handle. We ask them to clean our streets of drugs and violence. We ask them to referee domestic disputes. And we also ask them to deal with the people nobody seems to want to deal with, the mentally disturbed. To get a look into the job of modern policing let's take a look at what's happening in one our major cities today, the city of Chicago. To put it bluntly, Chicago is a mess. The murder rate is skyrocketing. There were 762 murders in Chicago 2016, up from 468 in 2015. When compared to other big-cities like New York and Los Angeles, Chicago had more murders than those two cities combined! When you combine the murders with non-fatal shootings, the figures in Chicago rose from 2,426 in 2015 to 3,550 in 2016. The Chicago Police report the vast majority of these shootings and murders took place in five Chicago neighborhoods. All these neighborhoods were poor and predominantly black with a very heavy gang presence. Over 80% of the victims in those neighborhoods were identified by police as having gang ties or prior arrests. The police are searching for solutions. The mayor, Rahm Emanuel, announced that he would be adding over 1,000 new officers to the department. So then why the spike?

There are those who feel that Chicago is not out of control, it's just those five neighborhoods spiraling out of control. Well, are they saying that those five neighborhoods don't belong to Chicago? Chicago without those neighborhoods is a really nice place? You better give precise directions to visitors then, you don't want them ending up in the wrong part of town, do you? Some would say no worries, they are just gang members killing other gang members. But what about the police of Chicago? How dangerous are their jobs today? Chicago police Superintendent Eddie Johnson had this to say about Chicago, "The truth of the matter is Chicago is not out of control. There's certain parts of the city that we have to address the violence." Well ok Superintendent Johnson, how will you address the violence then?

Mayor Rahm Emanuel linked the surge of violence in 2016 in part to the fallout from The Laquan McDonald shooting scandal that played out over 2016. Laquan MacDonald was a seventeen year-old who was shot sixteen times by a Chicago Police officer in October 2014. The officer in corroboration with several other officer accounts state that McDonald posed a danger and that the officer feared for his life. It took almost one year before the department was ordered to release the dash cam video taken that night from Van Dyke's police vehicle. In that video, McDonald is seen walking away, not towards the officers. He is seen with a small three inch knife in his right hand. The officer who shot McDonald, Officer Jason Van Dyke, exited his vehicle and within six seconds started to fire.

He was approximately ten feet away when he unleashed sixteen shots all within 14-15 seconds. Not one of the other eight officers who were on the scene that night fired a single shot. According to the Cook County Medical Examiner's Office's autopsy report, nine of the sixteen shots hit McDonald in the back and he was shot as he lay on the pavement. In November 2015, shortly after the release of the dash cam video, Officer Van Dyke was charged with first-degree murder in the shooting of Laquan McDonald. There was intense scrutiny placed over the Police Department which included a Justice Department investigation that wrapped up in January 2017. Some of the fallout from the investigation included exposing the Police Department's deteriorating relations with the city's minority communities. This fraying relationship combined with an ever dangerous gang environment, growing amount of guns on the street, and a Police force that has grown hesitant amid the glare of attention and criticism, are concrete reasons for the rise of homicides and shootings in Chicago today.

So now the difficult question is, how do we get this under control? Some in Chicago think it's an almost impossible task. But first, getting guns off the street can't hurt. Chicago had the highest increase in both homicides and shooting victims than any other major city from 2015-2016. An increase of 57% in homicides, and 46% in shooting victims. So a crackdown on criminals with guns is sorely needed. To the credit of the Chicago P.D., they took over 8,300 guns off the streets in 2016.

Back in the 1990's during the height of the crack epidemic, Chicago's drug trade was ruled over by two rival gangs, The Vice Lords and the Gangster Disciples. This was also a time when Chicago was averaging over 900 homicides per year. As the crack epidemic came to a close, Chicago continually saw a decrease in homicides till this sudden upswing. The two notorious gangs have splintered throughout Chicago, with many smaller gangs controlling just several blocks. It's the conflicts over drug territories that has led to so much of the violence. Authorities feel the immediacy of social media has exasperated the situation with personal disputes and challenges by rivals posing a dangerous threat. Chicago police estimate that 75% of all the homicides committed in 2015-16 can be attributed to gang retaliations. But how do you break the cycle of gang involvement? Many of the current gang members come from families that have been involved in the gang culture their entire lives. It's all they know. It is also the only way for many to make money. Albeit easy money and deadly money.

Guns, gangs, poverty, a demoralized police force all equally contribute to this epidemic. It took years, maybe even decades to get to this point, don't wait for a quick solution. It will be a collaboration, with involvement from the community leaders, law enforcement, educational leaders, mental health agencies, and local business leaders all pitching in to bring this under control. Many would accept under control for now. Ending it might be a pipe dream.

Racism – This is the second side to the triangle. How does this contribute to the growing rift between the police and the communities they serve? This is a delicate topic. Many people have many different opinions on this matter. All the opinions seem only to divide rather than bring communities together. I know that not everything is black and white (no pun intended). For me it's important to listen to all sides, and if you listen closely, I feel that all sides have valid opinions at times. No side is entirely right or wrong. The delicate balance between shifting opinions is where most of the solutions lie. Although the acrimony between communities of color and law enforcement have been in the headlines as of late, it is a very old story that goes back many decades. On the plus side, many police departments across the nation have made great strides in the areas of technology, science and social justice. All of which have served to improve law enforcement. Police departments have begun to move away from a responsive model of policing to a more proactive model with the emphasis being to attempt to prevent crimes from happening. Of course, despite these advances and improvements in policing, the old calls of police racism continue to be heard throughout the country.

Here's some numbers: According to a 2014 Marist poll, 76% of African Americans believed "there were problems in our justice system when it comes to law enforcement and race," compared to 33% of whites. Only 22% of African Americans have a great deal of confidence in law enforcement compare to 50% of whites. When looking at people of color, they are overrepresented throughout the criminal justice system. 60% of the total prison population in our country is made up of people of color, yet they only represent 40% of our total population. African Americans make up 13% of our population, but 40% of our prison population. Here's a stat for you, 1 in 3 African American males born in 2001 will go to prison at some time in their life. That's some heavy shit. No? When I tried to research police shootings and killings, I was astonished to find that there was no official government database that tracks this accurately. I also found that I am not the first to be puzzled by this. News media organizations such as the Washington Post and The Guardian in the U.K. took it upon themselves to develop such a data base. The Washington Post tracked their data back to 2015 and has developed a comprehensive database. But what do we learn from this? Does raw data tell the whole story? What were the circumstances? What caused the officer to use deadly force? Was it justified? We should all know that data can be manipulated to tell whatever story we want to put forth. When I did my own research, using varied sources, this is what I found. When using the website Mappingpoliceviolence.org, I came across the following: In 2016, the police killed at least 308 black people. Black people are 3x's more likely to be killed by police than white people. In 2015, 30% of black people killed by the police were unarmed as compared to 19% of unarmed white people. 69% of blacks killed by police were suspected of a non-violent crime and unarmed. And this website claims that in 99% of all cases in 2015 no conviction of a crime was reached for any officer involved in the killing of black people. This is a grim tale indeed. The data says so, right? Dam, we must have a serious racist police problem in our country, huh? Well, others have a different take on the matter. The media and high-profile leaders have consistently ratcheted up anti-police rhetoric. Prime example is a New York Times editorial justifying the Ferguson riots. In the Times editorial they claimed, "the killing of young black men by police is a common feature of African American life and a source of dread for black parents from coast to coast." As far as our leaders, the New York City Mayor leads the band. Mayor Bill de Blasio, as he was leaving for a Washington D.C. summit on policing, told the assembled press that the "scourge" of police killings is based "not on decades, but centuries of racism." A few days later when a Staten Island grand jury declined to indict an NYPD officer for homicide in the death of one Eric Garner, de Blasio said he worries of the dangers his biracial son, Dante, faces from officers who are paid to protect him. Even Hillary Clinton chimed in as she ran for president. She said that the criminal justice system is rampant with racism. She said, " blacks are more likely than whites to be arrested, charged, convicted, and incarcerated for doing the same thing." Is this helping matters? In the case of de Blasio, he faced heavy criticism from the head of the police union and from the rank-and-file as well. Many blame his rhetoric for the killing of two NYPD officers who were ambushed as they sat in their patrol car. It was a random, wanton killing by an individual who stated on social media he wanted to avenge the deaths by police of Eric Garner and Michael Brown. Some union leaders accused the mayor of sending the message that police were to be feared and stated the blood of these two officers were on the hands of the mayor.

Fact is, when it comes to an officer's use of force, its crime not race that plays the biggest part. But if the narrative of racist police is said loud enough and repeated throughout our media, the elephant in the room, the propensity towards crime by young black men, gets drowned out. When you compare the violent crime rates among different races, young black men commit violent crimes at a significantly higher percentage rate than other racial or ethnic groups. Crime, by the way, is reported by victims not police. And the victims of young black crime are overwhelmingly black themselves. Police are having "police involved" confrontations with young black men because black communities are demanding protection. What if the police were to back out of these neighborhoods? What would the narrative then be? The racist police are turning their backs on crime? Racist police are turning their backs on its most oppressed neighborhoods, leaving it to wallow in crime, drugs, violence and hopelessness? And of course, the narrative would be that the racist police were the oppressors. The police are branded villains whether they are active or passive. It's not easy to be police today. And then some would say, it's not easy being black either. Which leads us to the final side of our triangle:

Policing - President Obama, in the face of growing tensions between police and the various communities that they serve, signed an executive order in December 2014 forming a task force on 21st century policing. The task force delivered its final report in May 2015. The purpose of the task force was to strengthen community policing and to rebuild trust between law enforcement and the communities they serve. This came on the heels of several incidents around the country which reinforced the need to forge lasting and healthy relationships between the police and the public. No small task indeed. The report centers around six "pillars": Building Trust and Legitimacy, Policy and Oversite, Technology and Social Media, Community Policing and Crime Reduction (always a good idea!), Officer Education and Training, and Officer Safety and Wellness. All good and worthy goals. But how was it received and how effective will it be still needs to be seen. An implementation guide was also produced to be used as a companion to the task force report. It's to be used as a tool in implementing the over 50 recommendations and 90 actions items found in the report. It addresses law enforcement, local governments, community members and other stakeholders who are interested in turning this report into a plan of action. It gives each group concrete ways to bring about change.

One member of the task force, Constance Rice, a civil rights attorney says, "The pillars that we laid out – those pillars are an absolutely great foundational platform for building the transformational plan that each department needs to go through." Do people actually talk like this? Oh wait, she's an attorney, never mind. Another task force member, Brittney Packnett, calls for patience, as she says, "We are dealing with issues that are deeply rooted in systemic racism and oppression and those roots go all the way back to the founding of our country...It's unrealistic to think that in a year's time we're going to uproot systemic racism and oppression." Ms. Packnett was appointed to the Ferguson Committee by Missouri Governor, Jay Nixon. The committee was established in response to the unrest after the shooting of Michael Brown by Ferguson Police Officer, Darren Wilson, and the subsequent looting and rioting that went on in Ferguson when a grand jury refused to indict the officer for his actions that night. Packnett is also involved in the activist group Black Lives Matter and has actively participated in numerous events such as the 2015 Baltimore protests, 2015-2016 University of Missouri protests, and the 2016 Donald Trump Chicago Rally protest. In 2015 *Time* magazine named her to a list of "12 New Faces of Black Leadership." *Ebony* magazine cited Packnett as well as other Black Lives Matters members to its 2015 Power 100 List for their work on Campaign Zero. What is Campaign Zero you ask? Glad you did. Campaign Zero is a police reform campaign launched on a website in August 2015. Campaign Zero has collected and proposed policy solutions and police reforms in ten different areas. The following are some highlights:

- **End Broken windows policing.** 3 major components.

    1. **Decriminalize minor crimes used to victimize African Americans.** Some examples are, consumption of alcohol on the street, possession of marijuana, loitering, and disturbing the peace. (I like my peace and quiet today. Kind of goes along with getting older.) Loitering, drinking beer and smoking pot on the street tends to get in the way. Believe me I would know. My crew growing up in the Bronx loitered, drank beer and smoked pot, and it disturbed people's peace. (Sorry, Mom.)

2. **End profiling and stop and frisk programs.** Establish enforceable protections from profiling people based on social, economic, or physical status. End predatory police practices, such as stopping someone who matches a general suspect description or furtive movements. (Kind of puts a damper on good police work, huh?)

3. **Set up new ways to deal with mental health crises.** Establish a response team that includes mental health experts as well as social workers and crisis counselors. (what a cluster fuck of competing voices that would create. "Excuse me sir, hold off on slicing that woman's throat till we can get our response team down here, please." Or "please hold off from shooting me until I can get the professionals down here to better handle this situation.")

• **Community Oversight.** 2 major components.

1. **Set up civilian oversight structures.** The Civilian Complaints Office would...resolve civilian complaints in a timely manner, swiftly respond to police shootings, recommend discipline to the Police Chief, investigate the Chief for corruption (I guess if he/she doesn't follow the recommendations), and be separate from anyone in the "police culture." (Their quotes, not mine.)

2. **Remove barriers to report police misconduct.** This would require the officer to provide the civilian with their name, badge number, reason for stopping them, and instructions for filing a complaint against them. (no instructions for obeying the law or where to send citations for bravery when they save your life?)

• **Limit Use of Force**

1. **Establish standards and reporting of police use of deadly force.** This would mandate officers to use deadly force only if there is an imminent threat to the officer or someone else's life and the force is unavoidable. An officer must give a warning and give time after the warning in order to get a response. (Hmm, why not ask the officers to shoot the gun out of the suspect's hand? Or just shot them in the leg? How much time do you give? I have never had a gun pointed at me, but I suspect time moves real slow, 5 seconds can feel like 5 minutes. Just saying. Watching too many cop shows.) The name of the officer and the victim (why the victims and not perpetrators?) must be released to the public within 72 hours. (Sure, and why not just give the public their addresses while you're at it? Because the public always acts in a calm and thoughtful manner, right?)

2. **End traffic related police killings and high-speed chases.** Officers would be forbidden to shoot at moving vehicles (even if the vehicle is coming straight at the officer?), block a moving vehicle, and engage in high speed chases with non-violent suspects. (well, if a non-violent suspect instigates a high-speed chase, isn't said suspect now considered violent? I don't know of many cases where the police are out in front of a suspect's car inciting a high-speed chase.) (Ok. So, if you have a kilo of cocaine in your trunk, but you are pulled over for not wearing a seat belt, all you have to do to avoid the officer finding said cocaine or even giving you a ticket is to speed away. Hmm, interesting

3. **Monitor Police Force and Increase Accountability.** Catalogue all use of force incidents. (no problem here, transparency only helps to shed light.)

- **Community Representation**

  1. **Proportional representation of officers in their communities.** Police departments must develop strategies and a timeline to increase representation of women and people of color in their departments. (Agreed. But standards must be kept. On the other hand, there is no room anywhere in our society for hiring standards that excludes based on gender and or race.)

- **Filming the Police**

  1. **Body Cameras.** Police officers would be required to have body cams and dash cams in their vehicles. Citizens would have the right to have footage released to the public and held for up to 2 years. * Here are some pros and cons when dealing with body and dash cams:

  Pros:

  a. A camera will definitely give you a clearer picture of what happened during an incident.

  b. It will improve behavior of both police and citizens. People tend to behave better when they are being watched. Officers will buy in once they see how frivolous complaints are resolved by going to the tape.

  c. It will reduce complaints and incidents of use of force. For example, the Rialto, Ca. Police Department found a reduction of 87.5% in officer complaints, as well as a 59% reduction in use of force in just one year.

  Cons:

  a. Upfront costs. Cameras can range from $399-$599 per unit. Do the math, expensive for big city departments. NYPD for example, has over 34,000 uniformed officers.

Quick math on my calculator says that's an expenditure of over $13.5 million, if you use the low end. The NYPD has an operating budget of $5.2 billion, cameras would account for approximately 2.6% of that budget.

b. Privacy concerns. This means the privacy of the citizens themselves. There is a delicate balance between a person's Fourth Amendments rights vs. a public's desire for transparency. Will the officers have the right to turn off the camera in sensitive or potentially dangerous situations? Might negate the whole idea of having a camera.

c. Storage of evidence. What's most important is the chain of custody. When the evidence is taken to court, can you prove where the evidence has been, and can you say that it hasn't been tampered with? There would also be an additional cost for storage hardware or cloud-based storage systems.

This leads us to the Black Lives Matter movement. The Black Lives Matter movement, not moment, as it points out on its webpage, was created in 2012. It was created in response to:

"…Trayvon Martin's murderer, George Zimmerman, was acquitted for his crime, and dead 17-year old Trayvon was posthumously placed on trial for his own murder."

The organization was founded by Patrisse Cullors, Opal Tometi, and Alicia Garza. Three women with real passion for their cause. Whatever your feelings are towards this group, it has been successful in getting the attention of the mass media and America at-large. Opinions are all over the spectrum. And opinions are heated. Some say that the Black Lives Matter group should be considered a hate-group. Hate toward the police. They claim that the group legitimizes and enables anti-police violence. There has been a rise in All Lives Matter and Blue Lives Matter groups. Many critics of Black Lives Matter point to the very real situation of black on black crime. Critics say the movement is quiet unless a black life is taken by the police. There are no protests or outrage when police have been ambushed and assassinated by those in response to perceived injustices cited by the Black Lives Matter group. In St Paul, Minn. Black Lives Matter protestors marched on a state fair chanting, "Pigs in a blanket, fry them like bacon." This coming only hours after the senseless assassination of a sheriff's deputy as he refueled his vehicle in the Houston, Texas area. Oh, and by the way, the protestors chanted this as they marched behind a group of police officers there for their protection. Black Lives Matter stayed quiet then and stayed quiet when other incidents of senseless violence and murder toward law enforcement took place. On one side, you have people praising the movement as one that focuses on anti-black racism in the U.S. as well as focusing on several high-profile incidents when unarmed black men have been killed by police.

They say that Black Lives Matter is a peaceful movement of men and women that are not saying that *only* black lives matter, but rather in a persistent environment of discrimination, black lives *also* matter. I can't argue with those with those beliefs. Reasonable indeed. But unfortunately for those who strive for peaceful change, there are those in their movement who favor a more radical approach with a more persistent strain of violence. Here are some examples from just one month in time:

- July 2016, in Dallas, a black terrorist opens fire on police killing five in the worst police massacre since 9/11. The man responsible for the attacks told police negotiators that he was upset about recent police shootings and that he wanted to kill white people, especially white police officers.

- July 2016, in Tennessee, black man opens fire from a highway killing a woman and injuring three people, including a police officer.

The shooting, he said, was motivated by police violence towards African-Americans.

- July 2016, Missouri, police officer ambushed by a man outraged over police actions towards blacks. The shooting left the officer fighting for his life.

As you can see, July 2016 was one deadly month for law enforcement. How did we get here? And who is to blame? Not easy questions. And I would suspect the blame falls on many different segments and people in our society. First off, we have to stop shooting cops. Nothing good can come from that. We need transparency in all police shooting investigations. No harm to anyone if the shooting is deemed justified. But with a cloak of silence, appearances are that there is something to hide. Never a good thing in any case. We need our leaders to get on the same page. Show the same remorse and outrage when law enforcement is killed or wounded as when others are killed. Leaders must show restraint before making any statements surrounding an incident. No room for politics and thoughts of reelection. If the officer is found negligent, prosecute them to the fullest extent of the law. No law-abiding officer would disagree. Bad cops make the job harder for good cops. And there is an overwhelming amount of good cops in our country. Men and women who do a difficult job, expecting to go home to be with their families at the end of their shifts. Personal accountability has to be involved as well. Running from police, committing petty crimes, being uncooperative only adds to the tensions that can exist in many situations. It's when we look at this from the three sides of violence, police and racism separately, do we begin to see the complexity of this situation. It's not enough to say that we are a violent society or that racism is at the core of all our problems or that it is the fault of our law enforcement agencies. We must address them independently to begin to address the problem as a whole.

CHAPTER FIVE

Education and Poverty

I t so easy for people to say, "if you want a better life, get an education". Many young people are now finding out that the promise of high paying jobs at the end of your educational career is just not there anymore. At least not there in the numbers we have become accustomed to. And we are talking about mainstream young people. Those who come from good educational backgrounds. School systems that are adequately funded. Colleges and universities of good standing. As a parent and an educator, maybe it's time to re-evaluate our thinking. Is the college route best for our students? Are there others ways to a path to success? And when you look at those outside the mainstream, the picture is extremely bleak. For those in poverty it's as though there is no hope. Now I know, there are those who are going to point to the small exceptions to this picture. They will preach about the children who have risen out of poverty to achieve success. Certainly that situation does exist, no denying that. But I might suggest that this is a tactic used to shift the focus from a very stark reality. Poverty and its prevalence in our society. And for the hordes of those who suffer from its grip, can education lift them up? Is there a level playing field? This chapter will examine the issue of poverty and also the issue of education in our impoverished communities.

First let's get some statistics out of the way. In 2017, in order for a single person to be considered in poverty by the federal government, they must earn less than $12,060. Read that again please. With my trusty calculator at hand, using a 52 week year, that comes to $231.92 per week. And with a 40 hour work week, that comes to $5.80 an hour. So according to our government, if you are single making $12,061 per year, you are not in poverty! Really? What world are we talking about? Take a look back at chapter two on the economy. Remember the pain the middle-class is feeling today? Well our current economy is just flat out crushing those in poverty. And the news is not any better for families.

Two people who earn below $16,240 are considered in poverty. Again, take a moment to digest that number. Going back to my trusty calculator, that's a whopping $312.31 per week, and $7.80 per hour. So if a young couple earns $16,241 per year, shit out of luck. You're not in poverty according to the federal government. Wow...WOW!! Now if said couple goes on to have two children the poverty threshold rises to $24,600 per year. That's $473.08 per week and $11.82 per hour. Earn $24,601 and you and your family have to make do with what you earn! Yay.

How in the hell does the federal government come up with these numbers? Well to begin with it was developed in the 1960's. And it set the poverty threshold at 3x's the cost of a basic food basket. Food in the 1960's was thought to account for approximately 1/3 of a family's cost of living. And nothing has changed since the 1960's, huh? Well at least the federal government has been kind enough to adjust the threshold to account for inflation. One problem with this is that in 2017, a family's food bill now accounts for only 1/7 of the cost of living. With this in mind, the poverty threshold should be 7x's the cost of a basic food basket. Nope. The federal poverty threshold is a flawed measurement in 2017. It fails to address the 21st century's family needs. It fails to consider nondiscretionary expenses such as; housing, childcare, out of pocket medical expenses, and transportation. Another important factor it fails to address is variations in the cost of living based on geographic locations. As if the good people of Sioux City, Iowa have the same living expenses as the people in Nassau County, Long Island. I looked it up, not that hard. It took literally two minutes. The cost of living in Nassau County, New York is 89.7% higher than the cost of living in Sioux City, Iowa. So if you were making $24,601 with your family of four in Sioux City and you move your family to Nassau County, you would have to find a job that earns you $46,671 to maintain that luxurious lifestyle you had in Iowa. Well the good news is that employers pay more in Nassau County. Not 89.7% more, but 30.4% more. So your job in Iowa would pay you $32,084 in Nassau County. You're $14,000 short of living that dream life you had in Iowa. And imagine the living conditions if you were to make $24,601 in Nassau County. The reason I use Nassau County is because that is where I live.

Let's examine what it takes to live where I live. And I'm going to examine a basic lifestyle, nothing extravagant. Let's talk about something called a living wage. This is the amount needed to live in the most basic of ways. Again we look at Nassau County. The living wage for Nassau County for a family of four is $29.72 per hour. This is almost 3x's the amount our government uses to decide who's in poverty and who's not. If you make $11.82 or below, there is help available from our government. But what about the untold number of people who make $11.83 to $29.72 per hour? On Long Island, the minimum wage is $11.00 per hour. It will raise by a dollar each year till it hits a high of $15 per hour in 2021. That is almost half of what is needed to maintain a living wage.

If you don't get sickened by the following statistics, then you miss the point entirely. In the great United States, the poverty rate is 14.5%, which translates to over 45 million people in poverty. That figure is up by 8 million from 2008. An additional 97.3 million people are considered low incomes which is income below twice the federal poverty level or $47,700 for a family of four. Going back to the living wage calculator, for a family of four in Nassau County, you would have to make at least $61,800 to give your family a basic lifestyle. This level of income only takes into account typical expenses. Expenses such as, food, childcare, medical, housing and transportation. Basic expenses indeed. No flat screen TV's, smartphones or Nike sneakers here. Basic expenses. When you look at the poor and impoverished here in the U.S. that comes to over 48% of all people. That's nearly 1 in 2 people. Chew on that for a second. The pain of the dwindling middle class is real indeed. We talked about it, and I feel it for real. But life for almost half of our country is a true nightmare. Again this is in the US, not some third-world nation. Wow. Makes me sick to my stomach. Now I can hear some people saying, the poor are lazy, drug addicted burdens who don't deserve our help. Well for some, that may be true indeed. But for the great majority, these are hardworking people, who get up every morning and go to work only to fall woefully short when it comes to taking care of their families.

A recent study found that there isn't a single congressional county in America where people making minimum wage could afford a two-bed-room apartment. Heck I make much more than poverty level and I can barely afford a two-bedroom apartment. In our country today there is a rapid growth of unstable low income jobs. And a failure of fulltime work paying family supporting wages. I know how hard it is to support a family. Most of us do. I can't imagine how debilitating it must be to the psyche to work hard in a 40 hour work week and not come close to supporting your family. Working poverty has increased dramatically over the last three decades. It was about 7 million in 1980, and today that figure is over 12.5 million. What does all this mean? The mere promise of work is an important factor in the American Dream. Come to America for a better way of life. Well, not so much now. I think most Americans would say that for any family that works fulltime year round, they should be earning enough to provide for their families. No? The numbers of the working poor have steadily increased since 2000, a disturbing trend and a signal for change. A change in policy that ensures all work pays a fair wage in the 21st century. How did the increase in working poor come about since 2000? Well it can be explained by the fact that over the last several decades businesses have generated a disproportionate amount of low paying jobs, coupled with the fact that wages have been flat for all but the highest earners during this time period. When you add the ramifications associated with the Great Recession (wages pushed down even further) it's a dim picture indeed.

The real victims of such poverty are kids. They are born and raised in this environment and it extends to all aspects of their lives. The two areas that have the most adverse effects upon poor children are lack of proper healthcare and proper education. For the purpose of this book, I will concentrate on poverty and education, but as you will see, many times the two will overlap, especially in early childhood.

Education reform has been a hot topic in recent years. Politicians get involved. They proclaim that they have the answers. Usually those answers concern more testing and more result-based evaluations of both teachers and school districts. But the one pervasive problem that faces public schooling today is rarely discussed and in many cases isn't even considered an educational issue at all. With recent data that shows that a majority of students living in western and southern states attending K-12 live in low-income households, now more than ever it is primetime in looking at how poverty affects education. Especially early childhood education.

- Poverty influences a child's cognitive capacity. Cognitive capacity isn't only influenced by genetics. Prenatal drug use, environmental toxins, poor nutrition, and the effects of stress and violence play a big part in the development of a child as well. All of these negative influences are all present in low-income households.

These children start their education behind the eight-ball. No pun intended. There is no level playing field for these children.

- A study done in 1995 by Hart and Risley showed that by the age of four, children from low-income families have heard 32 million less spoken words than their more well off peers. More recent studies show that the quality of conversations differs as well. I have to admit, I was skeptical at first as I'm sure some of you are now. But as I examined the study more closely, I became a believer. It is shown that parents with higher education and income levels engage their children on higher thinking levels which precipitates a more creative response. Parents in poverty lack the time and energy to go beyond simple and goal-oriented commands. This is a distinct disadvantage for children born into poverty.

This all happens way before a child walks through the doors of a school. Another study done by the American Psychological Association caught my eye. The study examined children who were both in poverty and suffered neglect. In total 65 children were studied. There were 23 girls and 42 boys. The mean age of the children was 11 years old. All the children were raised in public schools and all the children were on Medicaid. All had some reported case of neglect (physical, sexual and emotional abuse). All of the children had Department of Health and Human Services or Child Protective Services involved in their lives at some point. Some children experienced multiple instances. In most cases the children were removed from their home environment where the neglect was occurring. Here are some findings:

1. 33-56% of the children performed below average in academic ability. I'm amazed the numbers weren't higher. But up to more than half of these children will suffer academically. And folks, it's not that they are not trying hard enough, or they don't care.

2. 60% of this test group will more likely be diagnosed with developmental delay. (compared to 10-20% outside this group).

3. 80% will have ADHD (look it up), compared to a "normal" range of 3-7%. 80% to 7%!!

4. 28% will have LD, compared to 5%.

5. AND 100% had emotional/behavioral disorders, as opposed to 46% outside the group. They are not savages, they are not disrespectful. They are poor. Plain and simple. Poverty has a direct link to your ability to think, memorize, synthesize information, and perhaps most importantly, how to act properly.

The study goes on to suggest the likelihood of long-term implications both educationally and occupationally. The little boy or girl in that control group will grow up disadvantaged, and guess what? They will live in poverty and raise another generation of disadvantaged children. Hasn't this gone on too long already? Reason suggests that to improve outcomes for low-income children, programs and policies used early, early as possible, may break or at least lessen links between poverty across generations. Its income levels folks, NOT RACE!! Enriching a child at any point in development can make a difference in his or her abilities. Income and educational levels shape human development. The case for investment in society's poor children is very strong.

Now for the big-boy decisions. Does money really matter for low-income children's outcomes? Well one word, YES! Money is needed to raise household incomes, more money is needed in our inner-city schools, and programs are needed to improve parenting skills. Skills these parents didn't learn because they were the prior generation's disadvantaged kids. Strong evidence shows as income increases, educational attainment rises along with it. And something else occurs, crime goes down. Funny how that happens, huh? Next I'll be talking about violence and drug dealing on the decline. Crazy talk!

Money is needed for mental health services and after school programs. This is a time tested method to increase school attendance, grades, and those beloved assessment scores, as well as a reduction in behavioral problems in students. Kids act better when their lives are more stable. I saw a definition of what poverty really is and I want you to read it and put yourself in the shoes of a young child or young teen:

> *"Poverty is the unrelenting daily task of trying to make ends meet. It is the daily stress and worry if the car will break down or someone will get ill or your child will need a new pair of shoes. And then having to choose whether to pay the rent, pay for medicine or pay for food. Which necessity will have to be sacrificed to pay for the added expense of the unexpected bill? Poverty is the exhausting, unending, time-consuming struggle of juggling and just hoping to make ends meet with no end in sight. Poverty robs you of a sense of security and it destroys your self-esteem and your hope for the future. And it has the potential to be hereditary..."*
>
> POVERTYPROGRAM.COM

Whew. Hits me right in the gut. And do you think the children feel their parent's stress and tension? Do you think that perhaps they take on this stress with their yet to be developed brains and bring it to school? Or the streets? This situation is here folks, and it's only getting worse. Some more stats to make you puke:

- Over half of all Americans will live in poverty at some time in their lives.

- Nearly one-in-six Americans live in poverty today.

- US poverty rate grew at twice the rate of US population growth.

- Poverty among the elderly has risen by over 20%.

- US has the highest number of billionaires in the world.

- One in every three billionaire lives in the US.

Now stats for children in poverty:

- One in four children live in poverty with nearly 200 million children receiving free or reduced price lunches.

- One in four children run the risk of going hungry.

- Less than half of the children receiving free or reduced price lunches head to school with a breakfast in their bellies.

- Children are the largest population of poor in our nation.

- Half of all US children will eat meals paid for by food stamps at some point in their childhoods.

How about this tidbit from the American Medical Association's Archives of Pediatric and Adolescent medicine:

> *"American children face the highest levels of poverty and social deprivation of any children growing up in Western developed nations, and they have the flimsiest social safety net to fall back on."*

- UNICEF found that when dealing with child health, the US ranked second to last among all industrialized nations of the world. Take a moment and read that again.

This won't end folks. It's here, it's real, and I say it's about time we did something about it. Now I don't have grand aspirations of leading a movement to overhaul our thinking and our policies here in America. It took generations to get here, it will be time before we get to the real solutions. We most certainly won't get there if we get distracted by the people who can be agents of change. You know those people, the ones who stir the racial pot, the immigration pot, the Black or Blue Lives Matter pots, and any ole pot that distracts us from the real culprit here. The rich are getting so F'ning rich while the vast rest of us are drowning in debt or barely spinning our wheels. Get the minions fighting amongst themselves and they won't realize we are robbing them blind. That's their thinking, and it works to perfection.

Now I would be negligent if I didn't at least offer up a path out of this mess. The following are my keys to ending poverty:

- **Improve education** ~ for both are children and also for adults. $$$

- **Affordable healthcare** ~ Medicare for all?

  - Now I know this is a controversial concept, which is trumpeted by Bernie Sanders. But at some point we will have to put aside the noise drummed up by our political parties and listen to what might be best. Remember what I said earlier about the agents of change distracting us from the real problems? Well is there a larger pool of agents of change then OUR ELECTED officials? Should it matter which side of the aisle proposes a plan, if it can help us rise up? We are currently in a battle of the ages involving the Pro-Trump and Anti-Trump factions. The noise is deafening. Who is benefiting? Certainly not the people who need the help the most. So why not try change?

Here are some Pros and Cons to Medicare for All or a single payer system as it is sometimes called:

Pros:

1. **Everyone would be covered.** In this single payer system, healthcare is viewed as a right, not as a privilege!

2. **It would create spending leverage.** By using a single pool of cash, it allows for negotiating for lower rates. The cost for providing care for many services could go down as a result.

3. **Private care can always be made available.** You want to go outside of the system, go ahead, it is America, isn't it?

4. **Here in the Great U.S. of A, we already have a system in place.** Medicare and Medicaid are single payer systems that cover specific groups of people instead of the whole population. Senior citizens, young children, and those with real low incomes are the groups now involved in a single payer system. Converting to a system for the entire population using the already existing structures would make the conversion substantially easier.

5. **Health insurance costs go away.** Although the tax rates are higher in countries with a single payer system, there are no healthcare payments to be made either. The guarantee of universal coverage makes the slight increase more palatable. And for those families paying $600 or more per month, there might actually be a savings.

Open minds folks. Think outside the comfort area. Ask yourself if the current state of affairs in our country is making life easier for you, or is everything more difficult?

Cons:

1. **Medical providers may opt for private-pay only, unless legally mandated otherwise.** For many, if not all medical providers, the thought of making less money under a single payer system is just not appealing. The government would have to mandate that care options continue to be provide for all.

2. **The single payer system does not solve the doctor shortage problem in the U.S.** Forbes Magazine reported in a 2016

article that the U.S. would suffer a doctor shortage by 2025 of up to 97,400 doctors to care for an aging population. A lack of access in some areas would still exist with a single payer system. Come on kids, we need more doctors!!!

3. **The money for a single payer system has to come from somewhere.** For countries who already have a single payer system in place, the pool of cash needed comes from taxation. Here in the U.S. we already see this with the Medicare/Medicare salary withholding. Corporate and sales taxes can also rise, along with taxes put on gasoline to pay for this system.

4. **It increases the size of the government.** This is seen as a big drawback for a single payer system. Adding additional layers of bureaucracy can lead to increased wait times for services for those who are in need.

5. There might be a reduced effort to innovate. Competition fuels innovation. In a single payer system you eliminate completion therefore innovation might suffer and the quality of care can be reduced. There is always the private pay sector, but can end up being too costly for the average earner. Paying for both the single pay and private pay systems would just be too much.

I never said it would be a simple fix, but Its an idea that's out there, and I think an idea that needs to be considered by our leaders.

- **Create jobs.** There is a lot of worked to be done in our country. Unfortunately a lot of that needed work doesn't generate profits. That is where the U.S. government can step in folks. Investments in infrastructure – building mass transit, fixing old bridges, converting to clean energy, also making needed investments in vital services such as schools, childcare, and elder care generate both

146

public benefits and much needed jobs. Building affordable housing provides jobs and also increases disposable income as housing cost would decrease. Free community college could train more people for our economy. And if you truly believe that everyone who wants to work should have a decent job, the government would become the employer of last resort.

- **Raise our freakin' pay!** The U.S. economy is fueled by more than 2/3 consumer spending. Fact is the GDP growth is chained to income growth. People can't spend what they don't have, and they don't have the home equity to borrow and spend. Most American have not had a real wage increase since 2000, and in the wake of the recession, corporate bosses have tightly controlled expenses, salaries being the easiest to control. This has served to boost profits and corporate bonuses. But at what cost my friends? Here's something to chew on, some American cities are as unequal in wealth as some African or Latin American cities. For example, New York City is said to be the 9th most unequal city in the world, and cities such as Atlanta, Miami, Washington and New Orleans had similar inequality levels as cities such as, Nairobi, Kenya, Abidjan and the Ivory Coast. Our income gap is the widest in over 70 years.

Large income inequalities result in the following conditions within a society:

- Health and social problems are worse.

- Child well-being is worse.

- The prevalence of mental illness is higher.

- Drug use is more common.

- Life expectancy is shorter.

- Infant mortality is higher.

- Obesity rates higher, educational scores are lower, teenage pregnancy rates higher and on and on and on.

Raise our pay!! In the late 1960's minimum wage could lift a family of three out of poverty. Indexed to inflation, minimum wage would be $10.86 per hour today. Today's current federal minimum wage is $7.25 per hour. Raising the federal minimum wage to $10.10 and index it to inflation would lift over 4 million people out of poverty.

- **Increase the Earned Income Tax Credit for childless workers.** Earned Income Tax Credit or EITC is one of the nation's most effective tool in dealing with poverty. In the calendar year 2016 it helped more than 6.5 million people including over 3 million children avoid poverty. Yet childless workers miss out on this benefit, because the maximum EITC for these workers is one-tenth that awarded to workers is not a substitute for the other.

- **Support Pay Equity.** With female workers making 78 cents for every dollar a male worker makes, action must be taken to ensure equal pay for equal work. Closing the gender gap would cut poverty in half for working women and their families. Paying women equally would come to an average of over $6,500 per year, lifting many out of poverty. This action would also add a half-trillion dollars to the Gross Domestic Product. **2017…OH BOY!!!**

- **Provide paid leave and paid sick days.** Chew on this folks, The United States of America is the ***ONLY DEVELOPED NATION IN THE WORLD*** without paid family and medical leave, and without paid sick leave. This makes balancing work and family without sacrificing needed income. Paid leave is a very important anti-poverty measure as having a child is one of the leading causes of economic hardship. Additionally, 4 out of 10 private sector workers and 7 in 10 low income workers do not have a single paid sick day. Disgusting! This puts people in the impossible position of giving up much needed income or their job all together to care for a sick child. The FAMILY ACT would be a step in the right direction. Come on people, the game changers are sitting on their hands, only removing them from their asses to collect more money for themselves. Enough hate, enough noise, enough distractions, enough divisive politics, SHUT UP and get the job done for all people!!! We as a nation are a disgrace, when it comes to addressing the needs of all people, except for the uber rich.

- **Create work schedules that work.** Low-wage and hourly wage jobs come with unpredictable and ever changing work schedules. I hear it now, "Hey shut up, you're lucky I am gracious enough to give you a job", right? Bad thinking, divisive thinking, thinking that doesn't work. We have to put an end to that, recondition our thinking, anyone who wants to work should have a job, and one that they are not at the mercy of the boss.

New thinking, positive thinking, productive thinking, and thinking that can work, if we don't listen to the noise machine, politicians. The fucking pie is huge, it's time to cut it up more equitably, and it can be done folks, we have to believe it can be done. Don't get distracted by the noise of divisive politics, because all it does is distract us from the real problems in our society. Poverty is not inevitable people. Don't believe that lie. We just need to develop the political will to enact the policies that will increase economic security, expand opportunities for all, and expand the middle-class!

CHAPTER SIX

Hold On to Your Seats, Folks

This brings us to a man who needs no introduction. I am writing this as President Donald J. Trump finishes his first full year in office. And boy, what a year. In my lifetime I have never seen a more polarizing figure. His enemies are many, and his supporters are fierce and loyal. Like it or not, he is **your** president, and he will be for the unforeseeable future. Let's look back at the path taken by this man to win the highest seat of office for any man or woman on the face of this great, somewhat green, earth of ours.

On June 16, 2015, Donald Trump announced to the world his intentions on running for the presidency. The presidency of the United States. Yeah, the loud, boisterous, "look at me" guy who appeared on television saying, "you're fired" announced his intentions of running for the presidency. The presidency of the United States. Now, I don't know about you, but I have to admit, I was amused by this announcement, but at the same time a bit curious. The man who wrote the book, "The Art of the Deal" wants to lead the free world. Hmm. All told, there would be a grand total of 17 candidates declaring their intentions for being the next president. March 23, 2015 Ted Cruz officially kicked off the 2016 republican presidential primary by announcing his candidacy. He announces his candidacy in a speech he made at Liberty College, talking about the power of millions of conservatives rising up to reignite the promise of America. Fourteen months later, Cruz dropped out of the race. But what a fourteen months it was.

Donald Trump would be the last man standing for the Republican Party. It has been called by many the most unusual election in recent history. And it was unusual in so many different ways. Trump would probably call it simply the greatest, biggest, best election ever. In many ways Trump is right, he blew up the election process as we knew it. In 2014 the news was that maybe another Bush would be in the White House, or a Christie, or even a Cuomo. And for many the thought was that there was a very real possibility of another Clinton in the White House in 2016. Indeed Hillary Clinton got an early jump when several different groups organized behind a Hillary candidacy in early 2014. And this was even before Clinton officially announced her candidacy. Many in the Democratic Party worried that this early effort behind a Clinton presidency would take the focus off the 2014 Mid-Term elections when the balance-of-power in the Senate was very much at stake.

But I want to keep the focus on Trump, and examine how a million-to-one shot wins the 2016 presidential election. On that June day in 2015, Trump announced his candidacy in front of his Trump Towers (of course he did). He revealed his intentions to build a "great wall" at the U.S.-Mexico border. And he told the world he would get Mexico to pay for it. The biggest, best, greatest wall ever built, all paid for by Mexico. There is much debate and misinformation regarding what Trump actually said that day concerning Mexico and the Mexican people. Yes he said that Mexico is sending rapists our way, along with drugs and crime, but he did assume some were good people as well. His message struck a chord with many in our country who were looking for answers, and more importantly, scape-goats, someone to blame for the quagmire most of us were living in. Trump came off as a man of action, a man for the people. Some would say, what people? Others would say he speaks our language. He was not the cook-ie-cutter political candidate spewing the same 'ole shit we have heard for decades. For many he was a fresh voice, and quite frankly, he was voic-ing the things that many people have been secretly thinking themselves for years. While the other Republican candidates were too busy dismiss-ing Trump and his message, he was a runaway train going downhill. The other candidates mistakenly believed that his message was unsustainable. He was bound to crash and burn at some point. Opps. Gross underestima-tion people, huh?

On August 6, 2015 during the first GOP debate in Cleveland, Ohio, Trump defiantly stated that he would no way endorse a Republican candi-date, if that candidate was not him. He was not playing by the rules. He was booed when he made those comments, but he was starting to gain momentum and he was hitting on all cylinders right from the start. He was the cocky, arrogant, television figure we saw on his highly successful show, "The Apprentice." But it was after the debate that Trump would gain the most attention. He lashed out at one of the moderators, Megyn Kelly, for questioning him about inappropriate comments that he had made towards women in the past. Trump was quoted as saying, "You could see blood coming out of her eyes. Blood coming out of her wherever." Not exactly an Abe Lincoln, Gettysburg moment Don. But get this, on August 26, just twenty days after the first debate, polls showed Trump closing the gap between himself and Clinton. Her lead was now 6 points, whereas it was 10 points at the beginning of that month. Oh, and by the way, he was lead-ing all Republican candidates at this point. That noise you were hearing was the Trump runaway train. The biggest, greatest, loudest train we have

STEVEN SLATEST

ever seen. Or at least that's what Trump would say. Trump would eventually cave in in September and sign a loyalty pledge, binding him to endorse whoever wins the GOP nomination. It also put an end to any talk of a third-party run if Trump lost the GOP nomination.

So how did this man, who polarizes the country as no other figure I can recall, get to become our President? Some suggestions:

Social media

- Some analysts would point to social media, and Trump's effective use of the medium, as a reason for his unlikely victory. Just like Franklin Delano Roosevelt's use of the radio, and John F. Kennedy's use of the television, social media gave Trump the vehicle to drive his narrative. His message was played out all over social media for everyone to consume. He has an estimated 24 million followers on Twitter, over 20 million on Facebook, and another 5 million on Instagram. Let's remember Trump's background. He had multiple successful businesses. His empire was worth billions of dollars. (by some estimates anyway.) He was also part of a widely successful television show, *The Apprentice*. He fully understood the powerful leverage social media has well before deciding to run for president. Social Media would be the place where he could get instant reactions. He used this strategy to keep his name out there, and to also gauge how his message was being perceived and by whom. When it came to the general election season, Trump crushed Clinton when it came to the use of social media. Clinton might have come off more polished than Trump during the debates (debatable), but on social media where all the attention is, it was no contest. Hands down Trump. Television ads are a thing of the past. People watch Netflix, Amazon Prime, or Hulu. And if they watch conventional TV, chances are they are fast forwarding through those commercials. Social media is where they are soaking up the message. Trump got the message out, and it was picked up by every main stream media source as well. That was the winning formula to be sure.

• If you are going to use social media, you might as well be interesting! Whereas Trump was flamboyant, and some would say, over the top, no one would argue that he was successful. Trump is above all things, a businessman. He is the farthest from a politician that we have ever seen run for the presidency. Remember this is his first stab at running for any kind of political office folks. As a businessman he understood how a well-placed provocative social post would get the nation's attention, and have them talking about him. Lord knows, Trump love attention. Good or bad, positive or not, everyone was talking about Trump. If everyone was talking about Trump, who weren't they talking about? That's right, Hillary Clinton. Not to say that Clinton didn't use social media, because she did. But Clinton's use came off as every other politician who has used social media. That is, very politically correct. Others might describe her posts as boring, revealing nothing of how she really feels. Want to know how Trump really feels? Read his twitter account. Only problem is he might have several different feelings on the same topic to express throughout the day. He is a stream-of-conscience twitter user, so to speak. Some would describe it as diarrhea-of- the-mouth syndrome. (Or fingers as the case may be.) One major difference between the two presidential camps was that Trump was in full control of his social media accounts, maybe not always a wise decision, but he was nevertheless. Whereas Clinton had staffers who posted for her. Thereby they would edit and polish the message, usually in a PC fashion. Read Trump's posts, no editing. It's full of misspellings and grammatical errors. Another words. REAL. Not fake and robotic and politically correct. And apparently this is what a large segment of the electorate wanted. In fact the public ate it up, always wanting more. Trump was also willing to defend any of his controversial posts. In fact he welcomed the chance to defend any outrageous post made. That way he can have it re-tweeted throughout the country and even throughout the world. Clinton never had to defend her posts, because remember, her posts were boring and politically correct. They were sure not to offend or raise any controversy. Therefore Trump was always at the center of the social media world and Clinton got to watch from the sidelines. He controlled the conversation. Trump was a pioneer in the effective use of social media for winning the presidency. Let's see what happens in 2020, you think social media will be boring and politically correct? Doubt it very mush. Trump has brought the social media world to the front of the pack. Leaving the other mediums behind.

- Trump led the way. He was relentless. He would set the daily media agenda by posting tweets by 6:00am. Posting one provocative tweet after the other, feeding that ever hungry mainstream media beast. He had them following him all day, every day. He was in essence receiving millions of dollars of free media attention, and from the very same media that wanted to see him lose. This was part of the winning strategy employed by the Trump camp.

Low Voter Turnout

- Plain and simple folks, in the 2016 Presidential election, a lot of folks did not vote. Out of the entire American population of eligible voters, only about one-quarter (27% to be more precise) voted for Trump. Now anyone can play with numbers, so let me say that only 58% of the voter eligible population actually voted in this election. This means that 42% of people eligible to vote, simply didn't. The actual percentages for votes breakdown to a little over 27% for Clinton, slightly less for Trump. Remember Trump lost the popular vote, but of course won the majority of electoral votes needed to become president. Why the low turnout? This is an issue that has confounded experts for many years. The United States ranks 31 out of 35 countries for voter turnout based on the eligible voter populace. In the 2012 election, it is estimated that 129 million out of an eligible population of 241 million actually voted. Presidential elections have far better numbers than the off-year elections like the one we will have in 2018. The last off-year election (2014) saw a voter turnout of 36% of registered voters, and that has been the norm for a very long time.

But we are talking about Trump and the 2016 election. Maybe in another book we can discuss the reasons behind low voter participation in the United States. The 2016 Presidential election saw approximately 130 million votes casted. That's on par with 2012 (129.2 million), which is down from 2008 (131million). While President Trump and House Speaker Paul Ryan (R) will talk about overwhelming support for the president and his agenda, that is far from the truth. It was said that Trump's victory provided him with a mandate because America came together as one and demanded it. Again, far from the truth. Remember folks, Trump won the electoral votes necessary to win the presidency, but a mandate? The loser, Hillary Clinton, received more popular votes than him. Facts be told, Trump is indeed our legitimate president. He won the election according to our Constitution, but let's not talk about a mandate and how America rose with one voice. In an election where the winner didn't win the popular vote, it's hard to accept the idea that the President is granted a mandate. This is usually reserved for those who win a clear cut victory by a wide margin .There have been five Presidential victories by more than 20% of the popular vote. I would argue that that is a mandate. Not losing the popular vote. But I marvel at the Trump victory and how he achieved it. Trump was indeed successful in getting groups of people to the polls. His Electoral College win was mostly based on the fact that he was able to perform well in some very key Rust Belt states. He was able to win the previously Democratic states of Pennsylvania, Michigan, Wisconsin (by .7%) and Iowa. A very strong showing indeed. Trump's victory in the Rust Belt states were indeed a result of positive Trump tactics, but it was also the result of some very poor campaign tactics employed by the Clinton camp. Here's what it boils down to. Republicans in recent history garner on the average 60 million votes. If the democrats can bring out more voters, as they did in 2004 and 2008 (Obama) they win. If they can't like in the case of John Kerry and Hillary Clinton, they lose. Clinton actually had 6 million fewer votes than Obama did in 2012 and 10 million fewer than what he had in 2008. So Clinton and the Democrats need to take a deeper look into that drop off. That's one hell of a drop off, from people who either were too uninspired to go out and vote for Clinton, and or who actually crossed the lines and voted for Trump. I would bet that people were uninspired and not so much crossing lines and voting for Trump.

Another reason cited for a poor voter turnout is that this was the first presidential election since conservatives on the Supreme Court gutted the Voting Rights Act. This allowed Republican controlled states to pass measures that would suppress the votes of those more likely to vote Democratic (African-Americans, Latinos, and college students). Some of these measures included strict ID mandates, limits on early voting, and reducing polling locations. They all seemed to have had its well-intended effect. In the very highly contested state of Wisconsin, where Trump won by 23,000 votes, over 300, 000 voters lacked the stricter forms of voter id's. This led to the lowest voter turnout in this state in the last 20 years. In the city of Milwaukee voter turnout was down 13 percent, where 70% of the state's African-American population lives. That's a whole lot of votes not casted. And if they were, it would be reasonable that those votes would go Clinton's way.

But let's move on. Analysts say that perhaps Clinton lost the election as much as Trump won it. Here's what Hillary Clinton said, "I take responsibility for every decision that I have made, but that is not why I lost." Really now? Your decisions had no bearing on your loss? She points to James Comey, the media, fake news (not only a Trump thing, huh?), sexism, and on the Democratic Party's infrastructure as the reasons she lost. There are two questions to be answered in my mind, (1) what caused Clinton to lose, and (2) more importantly, why was this election even close to begin with? Clinton indeed made mistakes. One big one was making and getting paid by Goldman Sachs to the tune of $675,000 for a series of speeches made to its executives in the fall of 2013. She claims it's sexism to bring this up. Nope, it's common political sense to stay away from Goldman Sachs if you want to run for president in 2016. She made the speech when she left her political post of Secretary of State in 2013, nothing illegal there. Short-sighted, yes. Illegal, no. This was during the time when our government was bailing out our financial sector, and it doesn't take a political genius to know that this just might look bad, and it will be scrutinized if you run for the presidency. It's not Sexism Hillary, it's common sense. I also don't buy placing the blame for her loss on a shaky Democratic Party or on her election team. Did Trump have a better team? Think again. There was far more infighting and leaking coming from the Trump team. Analysts say the Trump team made countless campaign mistakes. His finances weren't always sound, and his behavior was far more erratic. So then why did she lose?

Well first off incumbent parties rarely hold on to power after eight years in office. George HW Bush would be the recent exception (he followed the eight years of fellow republican, Ronald Reagan), but most would say that politics have become more polarizing in recent years. Hillary's husband Bill ran on the mantra,"It's the economy, Stupid" in a surprise victory in 1992. Hillary should have taken a page from his playbook. Her Democratic predecessor, Barack Obama guided the US economy from its financial crash in the early 2000's to a record series of numbers of quarters for job growth. 75 months of consecutive job growth to be exact. A modern record. Here's where Trump showed his guile. His message was one of stagnant wage levels, which I went into great detail, and the growing inequality of wealth here in the US. That's what the American people heard. Clinton failed to carry the message that the Democrats had some positive actions involving the economy. Score one big check for the Trump campaign. He harped on rigged trade deals, negotiated by former presidents and also talked about a rigged economy. This is what people who vote wanted to hear. Finally a candidate was talking the language of the working people. Clinton had no rebuttal.

Clinton suffered greatly when it came to the issue of trust. The Goldman Sachs speech, and murky ties to her family charity, left people questioning Clinton's words on money matters and basically anything else. It's hard to out shady Trump, in my opinion, but Clinton had that talent. And folks, let's not forget that cloud hovering over her head. God knows Trump wouldn't let you forget, and rightfully so. The cloud was the FBI investigation with possible criminal charges for her relaxed practice in dealing with data security laws as Secretary of State. This would all come to a head when the then FBI Director James Comey, sent a letter to Congress on Oct 28th, 2016. This was only a couple of weeks before the general election. The letter stated that the FBI had "learned of the existence of emails that appear to be pertinent to the investigation." The investigation was the one that was looking into the private email server of Clinton when she served our country as Secretary of State. The effect of this letter was plain to see. It may have shifted the race by as much as 3 to 4 points in Donald Trump's way. Analysts were saying that it swung the states of Michigan, Pennsylvania, Wisconsin, and Florida in his direction. Along with perhaps North Carolina and Arizona as well. Now some would say what's 3 or 4 points? Remember, Trump won the states of Michigan, Pennsylvania and Wisconsin by less than 1 percent. So some would argue that the letter was very influential in costing Clinton her victory in the Electoral College. 46 electoral votes up for grabs, 46 electoral votes Trump's way! When looking back on national polls conducted during the month of October, 2016, some polls had Clinton ahead by as much as 11 points (CBS Oct 12-16, 2016). USA Today had Clinton ahead by 10 points in a poll conducted from Oct 20-24, 2016. A CBS poll taken after the Comey letter saw the Clinton lead shrink to 3 points. (CBS Oct 28-Nov 1, 2016) That's an 8 point drop nationally. But who believes in polls, right? Certainly not Donald Trump. As late as the first week in November, Trump was given about a 15% chance of winning this election. But nobody wins elections in polls or before Election Day folks. What Clinton underestimated was the vast amounts of undecided voters in the swing states. And even if she was leading in the polls, she rarely polled over 50 percent in any of the polls. Turns out the Midwest had the most say in this election. Sure she had the coasts (California and New York) and with those states came a ton of popular votes. But it was Trump winning the swing states, no matter how small the margin that led him to his victory. Win by a vote, and win all the electoral votes!

And people had doubts every step along the way to Trump's victory. Going back to the beginning few thought he would ever run, but he did. Few thought he could climb up the polls, but he did. There was doubt as to his chance of winning any primaries, but he did. The Republican nomination, he did. But no way can he win against Clinton and become President of the United States! I still have trouble wrapping my mind around that! President Donald J. Trump. Our nation is sharply divided along educational, cultural, racial and ethnic lines. And there are probably more lines you can point to. Some I have already discussed in earlier chapters. We have so many people fed up with what's going on here. So much so that people were willing to let a man with ZERO political experience, and ZERO military experience, become our President. Some would say, why not, the political establishment hasn't done squat for us. Maybe the Don can get it done! Others would say, holy shit, what have they (the Electoral College) done? But really, has the same old shit worked?

The one group of voters who threw their support Trump's way was the working class. The people who get up every day, trying to stay afloat, trying to provide a life for their families. This is the group I talked about earlier who have been left behind. Feeling the weight of the world on their shoulders. Crying out for help, and Trump played right into their pleas. In our mainly white working-class counties across our country, voter turnout was especially impressive. Some of these counties supported Obama in 2012, but Clinton was unable to connect to these disenfranchised voters, and Trump did in a big way. These are people who are too busy at work to attend protest rallies. They are the backbone of our country and Clinton simply missed it. Or maybe she just didn't get it. Some estimates put the numbers of white men without a college degree voting for Trump at a whopping 72 percent. Taking a county in Michigan to use as an example, Macomb County is your typical white working-class county. In 2012 they threw their support to Obama over the home-grown Republican candidate by four percentage points. Not in 2016 folks, Trump won that county by 11 percentage points over Clinton. That is a fifteen point swing in the direction of Trump. Think he hit a chord? Maybe they felt left out or overlooked by the party they voted for in 2012?

Clinton did win the African-American and Hispanic votes in 2016, but her margins there were less than the margins achieved by Obama in 2012. One group that was a disappointment for Clinton was the college-educated suburban women. Not that many defected to the Trump campaign, they simply decided to stay home. Also the expected numbers of African-American voters were down as well. Maybe voter-suppression, or maybe just plain old apathy. Clinton's inability to motivate her voter base. Trump tapped into his in a big way, whereas Clinton had trouble tapping into hers.

We live in a big country folks. I live in New York, and I have to admit, I sometimes forget the vast middle of our country. Trump didn't. His win in Middle-America earned him the 2016 election. Trump spoke to the middle by telling them what they wanted to hear. For one thing, he acknowledged they existed. They turned to Trump to help restore the past glories of the steel and car manufacturing industries, what used to be the backbone of our great country. It is also the sector of our economy that just picked up and left. And with it the jobs of the people left behind. They were screaming to be heard for quite a while. Trump spoke to them, he told them (Detroit News, September 3, 2016) he would begin to levy a 35 percent tariff on all cars made in Mexico and shipped to the United States. Big applause, BIG APPLAUSE. He told a rally in Virginia that he would make Apple," start building their damn computers and other things in this country." More big applause, BIG APPLAUSE! His camp heard it, Clinton's turned a deaf ear. He also churned up an anti-Clinton feeling by pointing to her support to the North American Free Trade Agreement. An agreement that Trump said destroyed the industries that used to flourish in these now deprived areas. HUGE APPLAUSE. Blind faith on these voters part, since Trump never outlined a real plan on how he would achieve these goals. But someone was listening to them finally. And Clinton didn't hear it?

Let's take a look at the Electoral College. I teach middle-school U.S. History. I thought my head would explode when I was explaining how the Electoral College worked in our country. But folks, let's face it, not many adults actually realize how it works as well. Part of the reason why our brilliant founding fathers put the Electoral College in place, was to prevent the larger states and cities in overwhelming the less populated areas of our country. For example, the Democrats generally control the two big states and the large cities within in them that are located on either coasts. By dominating both California and New York, a shit-ton of popular votes go their way as well. The Dems have won the popular vote in the last six of seven elections. But yet they have managed to lose two of those elections. The power of the Electoral College. Get over it Dems, that's how we elect our Presidents. Figure it out, or continue to cry. It makes my stomach turn when I hear people, groups of people say, "He's not my president!" Get over yourselves, take out a book and educate yourself on what it takes to become President. He certainly is your President. And, if you don't change your thinking Dems, he will be till 2024!

No doubt Clinton was the more seasoned politician. Starting with her eight years in the White House as the First-Lady, then her tenure in the United States Senate representing the State of New York, and her four years as Secretary of State for President Obama. But it seems that far too many people were tired of and ready for a change from the typical politician and politics that they have suffered through for the last several decades. Along came Trump and his zero political experience and connecting with people on a more human level. He was seen as the complete opposite to the establishment. A tired old establishment. Score one, a very big one for Trump in 2016.

Trump might be a neophyte in politics, but he is a master in being in the public eye. As a New Yorker, Trump has been on my radar for a very long time. Decades. He has learned to let things just roll of his back. Scandals don't bother him. He has certainly seen his share, but yet, President Donald J. Trump. The 2016 election season was no exception when dealing with Trump scandals. His boasting about making sexual advances towards women (caught on tape), his refusal to reveal his tax-returns, making the comment that not paying his federal taxes actually made him smart, and by saying that John McCain was not a war-hero (New York Times, July 18,2015) because he was captured, any one of them would sink a candidate. But the Teflon Don would shrug it off and move on. Despite all of this, the people largely ignored it and named Trump the President of the United States.

So there you have it. A man who at the beginning of the process was seen as nothing more than an annoyance by some, always underestimated at every turn, took down all the established, more politically seasoned candidates, and did it in his very unique fashion. Always loud, always bombastic, but obviously hitting a chord within many people in the United States in 2016. He outsmarted and outplayed them all. His use of social media has now set the tone for all future elections. It was not always easy (that's for sure) but it definitely sent a message to the Democrats, and that message better be heeded by them if they are to have any chance in 2020. Let us all take a deep breath, and just digest what happened in this election. Hillary lost folks, and according to the U.S. Constitution, fair and square. Move on, respect the office of our Presidency, and more importantly, support. People from the opposite side of the aisle, did the same for the previous eight years. You think it didn't tear them apart to see a Democrat in office? It's called politics. It has been going on since the election of our second President, John Adams in the election of 1796. Yes 1796. It was the first contested election, since Washington was unanimously elected in the previous two elections. Adams represented the Federalist Party, and some light-weight politician by the name of Thomas Jefferson, (sarcasm here) represented the opposing Democratic - Republican Party. Adams won by a slim margin in the electoral college (71-68 electoral votes). And get this, this election was before we passed the 12th Amendment, which allowed the Electoral College to choose both the President and Vice-President. Sooo, whoever came in second became the Vice-President. Can you just imagine an administration comprising Trump as President, and Clinton as Vice-President? I almost wish it did happen, just to see them side-by-side, just for shits-and-giggles.

But thank God, the 12th Amendment was indeed passed in 1804, and we live under the present system. To make a long-drawn out point shorter, GET OVER IT! Trump won and Clinton lost. You don't have to like him, but he is YOUR President, for better or for worse. I for one am anxiously watching for any positive changes that can come from this Presidency. I am here to support our country. This is what happens every four years. And for you spoiled, always come away with a trophy people, maybe this is a lesson in how to act in defeat. Holding your breath and whining just isn't a good look. You're unhappy, do something constructive. Screaming at the top of your voice that you are unhappy and he is not my President is immature and doesn't do anything positive for the future. Many of my life lessons were learned from defeat and disappointment. Come to think of it, perhaps all the most meaningful lessons come from that place. What I have learned as a young man, and it was taught to me by my parents and my coaches, "Win with humility, lose with grace, and do both with dignity!" Game, set, match folks!

EPILOGUE

Whew, quite the journey, huh? Seventeen years, chock full of activity behind us in this 21st century. Each and every topic covered in the previous pages, would be worthy of book all to itself. That was not my intention. I wanted to take the reader on a quick, concise account of what I felt (and that's always up for debate) were the more important events so far this century.

Our Presidential elections were quite newsworthy indeed. We elected two presidents who lost the popular vote, and sandwiched in between, we elected the first African-American to the highest office in the land. Now that's quite a start. I am very worried about the middle-class, if that class exists any longer. We need to address the burgeoning gap between the rich and the not rich. I truly feel that if nothing is done to fix our economy and increase the growth-rate in our economy, dire times loom ahead. President Trump won on the slogan, Make America Great Again, and I can only hope he can put us on that path.

The issues surrounding poverty and education are at a breaking point. Again as I discussed in this book, there are ways to do this, but do we have the political guts needed to make changes? It would help if people realize that the forces behind the control of our country initiate the chaos among the people. If they can get the masses to fight among themselves, to blame one another for the problems in our society, they get to continue to dominate. Folks, there is such an abundance of wealth at the top, and it gets bigger as the years go by. Your neighbor is not the problem. Neither is it "those" people on the other side of the tracks. It's those who control the wealth, those who are content on getting even more obscenely wealthy that is the true problem. Can this go on forever? What will happen if the masses wake up and realize they have been led by the nose? There is plenty of wealth in our country. Enough for the uber rich to stay that way for generations to come, and if it gets redistributed correctly, by investing in the middle class as discussed in a previous chapter, we can indeed, Make America Great Again!

I hope I have opened some eyes, made you think, and encouraged you to become motivated. Be an agent of change, not an agent of discontent. I truly love this country, and hope that the America that my daughter lives in as an adult is an improved version of what we have now. This has been a most satisfying project for me. I was able to get out some things that have been festering within me. It was painful at times, since it brought up some very raw feelings. And satisfying in the hope that I may spark some debate, conversation, and disagreement. I believe great things come from people with differing opinions. Our country was formed on the belief that everyone is entitled to an opinion, and the right to voice it. But our great country was most notably formed on the basis of compromise, and unfortunately, that principle has not been on display much this century. Sure our country's greatness shines in moments of great tragedy, but we need to heed to our great founding fathers who formed this great country on the very principle of compromise. We can do it, we have to do it. Peace out!